P9-DJA-330

3/94

NORTH AMERICAN
INDIANS

Norman Bancroft-Hunt

COURAGE
BOOKS

An Imprint of
RUNNING PRESS
Philadelphia, Pennsylvania

Canadian Representatives:
General Publishing Co., Ltd.
30 Lesmill Road, Don Mills
Ontario M3B 2T6

9 8 7 6 5 4 3 2 1
Digit on the right indicates the number of this printing

Library of Congress
Cataloging-in-Publishing Number
91-58800

ISBN 1-56138-123-3

This book was designed and produced by
Quintet Publishing Limited
6 Blundell Street
London N7 9BH

Creative Director: Richard Dewing
Designer: Stuart Walden
Project Editor: William Hemsley

Typeset in Great Britain by
Central Southern Typesetters, Eastbourne
Manufactured in Hong Kong by
Regent Publishing Services Limited
Printed in Hong Kong by Leefung-Asco Printers Limited

Published by Courage Books
an imprint of Running Press Book Publishers
125 South Twenty-second Street
Philadelphia, Pennsylvania 19103

060828

Contents

•••••••••••••••

Introduction

Tobacco pouch, Eastern
Dakota (Sioux), 1820–
1830. Tobacco was used
ritually to honor or appease
the spirit forces, and was
smoked on meeting and in
councils for friendship,
trust, and good-will. The
decoration here is of dyed
porcupine quills, white
beads, loon feathers, and
tin cone dangles, all
attached to buckskin.

T HE NORTH AMERICAN INDIANS hold a unique place
in most people's imaginations as a result of
being so familiar through the Hollywood movie
and the Western novel. The image from these sources,
although it is an enduring one, is restrictive and does
little justice to the great richness and diversity of
American Indian cultures.

This book attempts to show this diversity and con-
centrates on the period before the lives of these
peoples were disrupted by the European invasions of
their lands. The photographs, many of which have
never appeared in print before, have been carefully
selected, and nearly all the objects depicted are ones
made at the time of first European contact, before
trade goods began to supplant local materials.

The text is concerned with people who adapted to
environments that ranged from tropical to arctic, with
deserts, grasslands, forests, swamps, lakelands,
savanna, fjords, coasts, islands, and mountains in
between. Their ways of life, their beliefs, and the
relationships between members of the group and with
other people of their areas, reflect the variety of the
land in which they lived.

The economies of native American involved hunting
for both land and sea mammals, fishing, agriculture,
and gathering. There were nomadic, seminomadic
and sedentary lifestyles. In certain areas they organized great confederacies and city states; but
elsewhere were tribal groups, clans, and small
extended-family bands. The populations of these
different groups might vary from only twenty or thirty
people to several thousand. In their speech, too, they
showed tremendous differences, and at least 500
mutually unintelligible languages were spoken.

It can be misleading to refer to all these very different people by the single term "American Indians."
The word "Indians" was applied to them when
Columbus misjudged his whereabouts in 1492, believ-
ing he had found a new route to the Indies. The name
"America" was coined after Amerigo Vespucci, who
realized the land was a continent previously unknown
to Europe – he himself named it *Mundus Novus*, the
New World, in 1507. The term American Indian is
used here because it has come into general usage,
but this carries no implication of an overall cultural
uniformity. Nor does it reflect the way in which the
native populations think of themselves. For most of
them, their own tribal names translate into English
simply as "The People."

This book will provide some understanding of what
their cultures were like. At the same time, however, I
would ask the reader to bear in mind that the Native
Americans are still here and, although much has
been destroyed and many sudden changes have taken
place in the 500 years since Columbus, they carry a
proud heritage with them into the future.

CHAPTER ONE

The Desert Dwellers

View in Pueblo Acoma N.M.

Acoma, Pueblo, *c*1885. Acoma (Sky-City) is built on the top of a mesa that rises nearly 400 feet above the plain, and is located near the modern city of Albuquerque, New Mexico. This township has been occupied for one thousand years. It has changed little in outward appearance, and remains today much as it was when this photograph was taken.

◀ ▮▮ ◿ ▮ ▮◿ ◿
Kachina doll, Hopi, Poli Kachin Mana, 1930. The Poli Kachin Manas (Butterfly Maidens) appeared in fours together with a single male dancer, Poli Kachina, who danced in the centre of their line.

WHEN THE SPANISH EXPEDITION of Francisco Vasquez de Coronado entered the Southwest regions of what are now New Mexico and Arizona in 1540, it stumbled across civilizations that had been in existence since long before the founding of the Spanish Imperial Court. They passed the snow-capped peaks of the Sandia Mountains, beneath which Ice-Age hunters had camped 12,000 years before. The ancestors of the historic tribes of the region had planted corn at Bat Cave as long ago as 3,000 B.C. Both Acoma (called Sky City, for its magnificent location on the top of a high mesa) and the Hopi village of Oraibi could have laid legitimate claim to being the oldest continuously occupied village sites on the entire North American continent. The Spanish were unimpressed by what they found. They had traveled north from Mexico in search of Cibola, the fabled Seven Cities of Gold, and found instead villages of multistory apartment complexes built from dried clay, or adobe.

THE PUEBLO

The country of the Pueblo people, as Coronado called them, brought forth cries of dismay from the Spanish, who wore full armor and chain mail, and for whom the summer weather was unbearably hot. The land was arid, cacti and the razor-sharp leaves of yucca bushes tore at their clothing, and their way was often impassable because of deep chasms and gorges. When they became the first Europeans to see the Grand Canyon, they stood on its rim and bemoaned the fact the precious water they sought was far below and unreachable. Had they reached the river, they would have found the isolated Havasupai Indians, farming small garden plots of corn, squash, and beans on the canyon bottomlands.

These Indians, together with other small tribes such as the Yavapai and Yumans, continued the age-old farming-gathering practices of the Bat Cave occupants. The nearby Pima and Papago were also farmer-gatherers whose ancestors, the Hohokams, had tamed the desert by 600 A.D. with a network of over 250 miles (400 kilometres) of irrigation ditches along the Gila and Salt rivers. The Hohokams brought a quarter of a million acres under cultivation. Although prolonged droughts forced the Hohokams to abandon their great villages and fields in about 1450 and return to garden farming, the Pima and Papago were nevertheless the possessors of a proud and ancient tradition. Ranging around these groups were small nomadic bands with a well-developed hunting

LOCATIONS OF THE SOUTHERN DESERT-DWELLING INDIANS

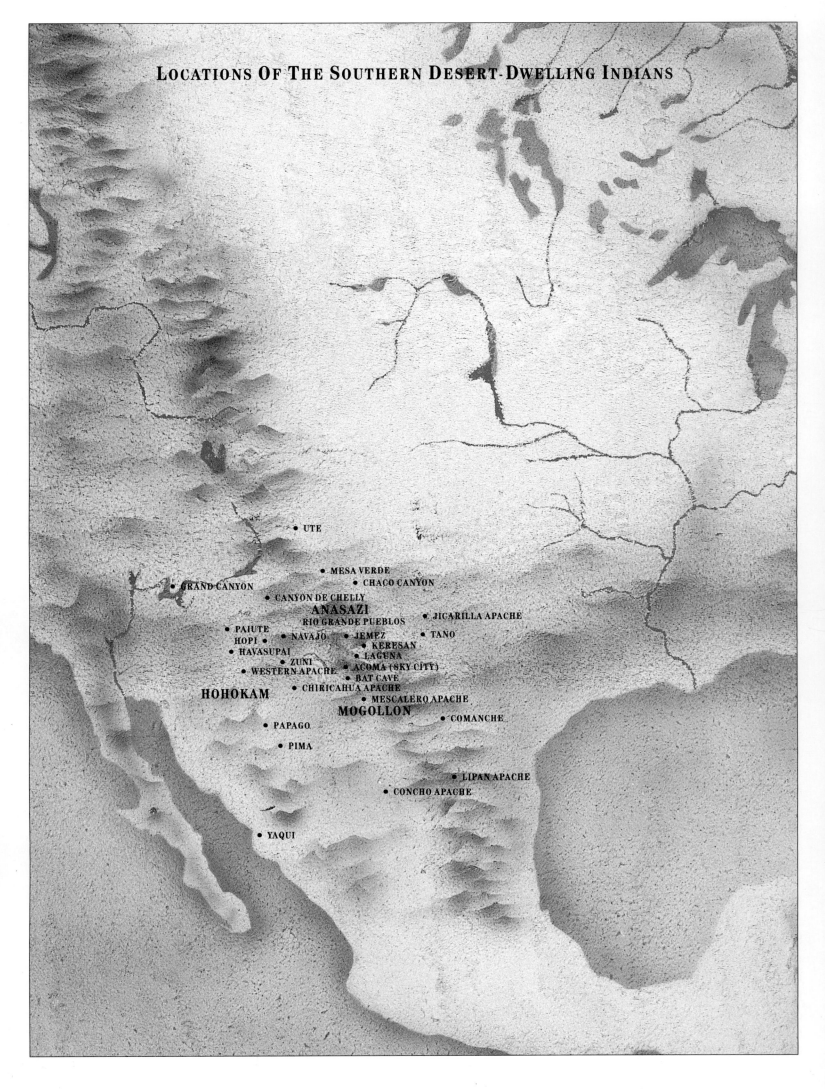

• UTE

• MESA VERDE
• GRAND CANYON   • CHACO CANYON
• CANYON DE CHELLY
ANASAZI
RIO GRANDE PUEBLOS   • JICARILLA APACHE
• PAIUTE
HOPI •   • NAVAJO   • JEMEZ   • TANO
• HAVASUPAI   • KERESAN
   • ZUNI   • LAGUNA
• WESTERN APACHE   • ACOMA (SKY CITY)
    • BAT CAVE
• CHIRICAHUA APACHE
HOHOKAM   • MESCALERO APACHE
MOGOLLON
• PAPAGO   • COMANCHE

• PIMA

• LIPAN APACHE
• CONCHO APACHE

• YAQUI

culture. These people were relatively recent arrivals in the area who had migrated from the far north. They were the Apache and the ancestral Navajo.

The Spanish reports of the time emphasize the harshness and difficulty of the Southwest and liken it to the dry, rocky regions of their own homeland. But for the people who lived there, the land had a deeper and generally more beneficent significance. Its chasms and gorges, instead of being impassable barriers, were expressions of the powers by which they had been created and formed. Its sandstone pillars and strange wind-blown rock formations were places from which the deities let down the web of life. Its colors were the inspiration for weaving and baskets, and its severity and discipline were a constant reminder that the people were subject to greater forces.

A LANDSCAPE OF LIGHT

Although the different tribes had lifestyles that ranged from sedentary agriculture to nomadic hunting and gathering, all of them were profoundly influenced by the mesas, canyons, and endless semidesert landscapes of the Southwest. The land is one of pure light, in which color and form are sharply delineated and thrown into sudden contrast, where one steps abruptly from sunlight into shadow. This is expressed in such bold and powerful art forms as Navajo blankets, in which geometric patterns echo the forms of the mesas and reinforce the people's link to the land. When Spider Woman first taught the Navajo women how to weave, she did so by creating her own designs from sky and earth, Sun shafts and rock crystal, lightning and rain; each Navajo blanket recognizes and recreates these original elements.

Pueblo potters took clay from the ground and fashioned it into bowls, jars, and ollas (pots) on which they created patterns of stunning delicacy. Rainbows, cloud symbols, and dragonflies, as well as the larger animals of the Southwest, are depicted with slow, measured lines that imbue the designs with a spiritual quality and give them a sacred significance. Image and background are sometimes deliberately confused to reflect the wholeness of nature, and as a means of capturing the essence that bound together the earth and the people.

The Pima, Papago, and Apache, although they had little weaving or pottery, employed the various reeds and grasses of their land in making baskets. On some baskets, maze and spiral patterns, expressive of the movement of rivers, give visual recognition to the life-giving qualities of water and reflect its importance in an arid area. Such baskets are painted with the colors of the desert, and the accuracy of their patterns and intricate weave blend the natural materials with the hand movements of the basketmakers. It is

almost impossible to look at such objects without understanding something of the calm consistency that has produced them.

THE SPIRITS

Every blanket, pot, or basket is a statement of continuity between object and land, and of the intimate relationship that existed between the people and the resources that their country had to offer. The forces that governed this relationship were never remote,

Acoma pottery ollas, late nineteenth century. The pots show a geometric style that has changed little over thousands of years. Acoma women are renowned for their thin-walled pots, made by a coiling technique in which successive "rolls" of clay are placed on top of one another and then smoothed out.

Zuñi eagle cage.   Hillers, ph

Zuni man with eagle, 1879. Eagles were sacred to virtually all American Indian tribes. This photograph includes an adobe and wooden-stake eagle cage at Zuni Pueblo. The young birds, taken from their nests, were reared in captivity so their plumage could be plucked for attachment to masks and rattles.

intangible elements that could only be invoked through ritual and ceremony. They were carried within all individuals and expressed through every aspect of their lives. For the forces to be brought into direct communication with the human world, they were personified in spirits such as the Kachinas of the Pueblos, the Yeis of the Navajo, and the Gans, or Mountain Spirits, of the Apache.

It was through these spirits that the life of the people was ordered, and the seeds for this were laid down in the distant mythological past. Among the Pueblo groups, which encompassed Hopi and Zuni, as well as a series of settlements in the Rio Grande Valley (known mainly by their Spanish names such as Santo Domingo, Isleta, San Juan, and Laguna, but also including Acoma), this past was firmly rooted among the mesas of the region. According to the Hopi, it was the Kachina spirits who guided the people

from a previous underground world, leading them through a hollow reed and by way of a badger hole high up in the mountains into the world of light they now occupy. Each *kiva,* or ceremonial clan chamber, had a small depression, the *sipapu,* marked on the floor to symbolize the original place of emergence. The Kachinas taught the people their ceremonies and gave them everything they needed to sustain life; they told the people that in all they did they should proceed with moderation and tranquility.

Because of this, life in the Pueblos was quiet and unhurried, marked by restraint, dignity, a sense of common purpose and an air of constancy and patient determination. For people such as the Hopi, the People of Peace, passive resolve was spiritually demanded and violence was anathema to them. A hand raised in aggression struck a blow against the natural order of their world. It was only if anger, loud words, and thoughtless actions came to the fore, creating argument and disagreement, that the integrity of the people, and thus their survival, could be threatened.

To avoid strife, the spirits divided the people into two groups and said that the Turquoise people would rule the Pueblo for half the year, while the Squash People would be responsible for the other half; but that all decisions were to be made jointly and arrived at through quiet discussion. Every aspect of life among the Pueblo was governed by the directives the Kachinas issued, but they, because they were spirit-beings, could not live permanently with the people. Instead they promised to return to the Pueblos for part of each year, and small cottonwood-root dolls carved and painted in their likenesses were kept in the villages year-round as reminders of their presence.

SPIRIT DANCES

Each year, when the Kachinas returned, masked dancers representing them performed in the plazas and *kivas*. As befits the Pueblo conception of communal cooperation, they danced in long lines of from twenty to sixty identical dancers. The dance was a measured and deliberate one in which the entire line would slowly turn from one side to the other, creating repetitive ripples of motion. This gentle rhythmic flow was intended as a representation of nature's own rhythms. It consequently reinforced the people's belief in these powers inherent in their land, while at the same time bringing these powers directly into the heart of the village. It was through this natural, unhurried motion that life-forces could be radiated and absorbed.

Although the Kachina dances were simple, they contained all-embracing truths. Through them the powers of the natural forces were unified and brought together as one presence, in which was represented every element of the plant, animal, and mineral worlds. A series of dances lasting throughout the winter "half" of the year retold the history of the people, beginning with the creation, followed by the germination of life, and finishing with its purification. Because the yearly cycle of seasons followed this same pattern, the dances also guaranteed that the rains would come and the crops would grow.

Everything a Pueblo Indian did reflected these unalterable sequences of life, and there was almost no activity that was not treated as a ritual supplication to the spirits and an acknowledgement of their power and presence. This resulted in a belief system that was highly formalized and very sophisticated, but which was inward-looking and allowed little deviation from its tenets. The Pueblo were, of course, aware that people living nearby had different conceptions. They traded with them and were often in close con-

tact. But the flow of influence tended to be from the Pueblos, and the introduction of alien elements to their societies was marked by its rarity. In some ways this has been very protective of Pueblo culture, and although most Pueblo Indians today are Catholic – seeing a confirmation in Catholic belief of many of their own legends – they still carry out ceremonies that are little changed from those being held when the Spanish first met them in the sixteenth century.

Hopi dancers, 1893. This photograph was taken at the Hopi village of Walpi. The foreground figures wear the costume of Hehea Kachinas, indicating that the Powamu (Bean-Planting) ceremony was about to begin.

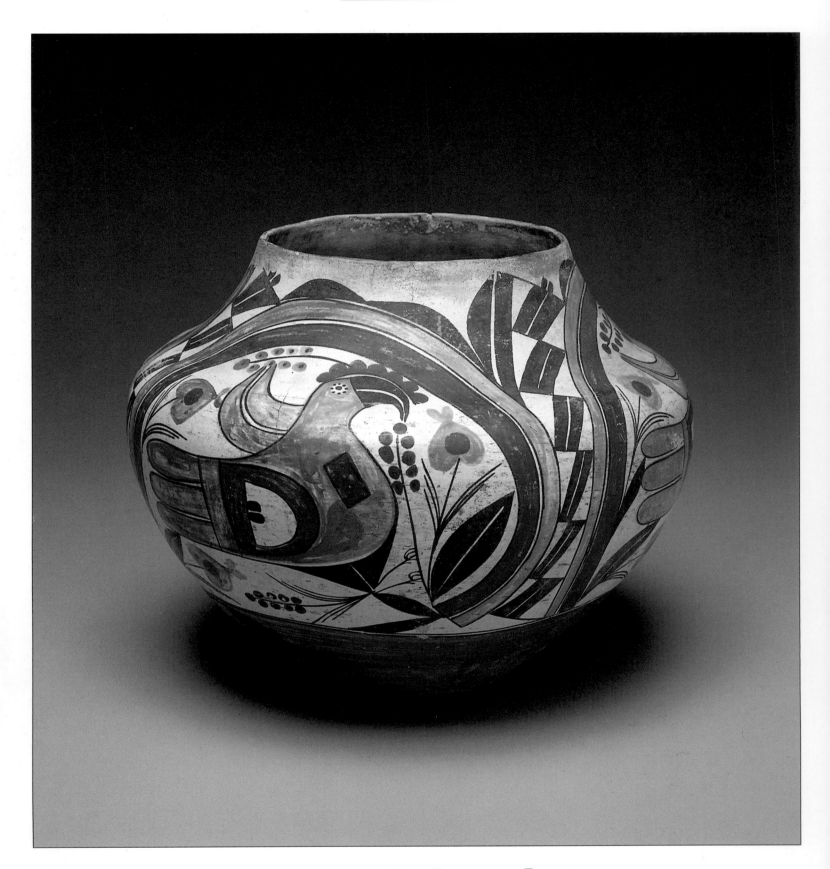

Pot, Chaco Canyon, *c*1000A.D. Depicting a bird figure, this fine pot comes from the ancient Pueblos. Chaco Canyon, northwestern New Mexico, had a complex of town sites, the Anasazi occupants of which were skilled potters.

THE PIMA AND PAPAGO

The history of the Pima and Papago in the Southwest is at least as old as that of the Pueblos, but they were more open to the ideas of other people. Even their Hohokam predecessors often shared village sites with the Anasazi ancestors of the Rio Grande Pueblos and the Mogollon ancestors of the Zuni. The Hohokam acquired the use of the *kiva* from the Anasazi, which indicates that they took over ritual ideas, too, and they used ball courts similar to those in Mexico. Other influences are apparent in the structure of their towns, with a central village serving as an administrative and religious focus for a number of surrounding suburban communities.

Like the Pueblo people, the Pima and Papago were essentially nonaggressive, quiet, and industrious tribal groups with a strong reliance on farming, which they supplemented with some hunting. Their homes, instead of being on the canyon rims and mesas, were

Pima-Papago women. Pima-Papago life centred on the products of the river banks and the various seeds, roots, and berries that these sustained. The women in this photograph are using large carrying baskets to transport what they have gathered back to the village.

located along the rivers that ran through the canyons. These rivers sustained extensive tracts of reed and tule (a large species of bulrush that grows only in this region) from which houses, mats, and baskets could be made. The rivers also supported the growth of grasses, willows, yucca, Devil's claw, and sumac, all of which were employed in creating exquisite patterns of light and dark in the basketwork at which these tribes excelled. Whereas Pueblo material culture reached its ultimate expression in pottery from the clay earth of the Southwest, that of the Pima and Papago is expressed almost entirely through the products of the river banks. The dependence on the rivers is reflected in the Pima's name for themselves, Ahkeemultootam, which means "River People."

MIXING OF CULTURES

Deep in the canyons, protected from the harsher extremes of the Southwest, there is a sense of isolation, since the soaring walls of the canyons present a barrier to life beyond their confines. For the Pima and Papago, this was allied with both a feeling of security and a need to journey to maintain contact with other groups. Such factors create a fluid society, one in which both social and ritual aspects relate to other people as well as one's own. A stranger is a welcome bearer of news and ideas from the outside, rather than an intruder whose different views might disrupt an established order.

Because of this openness, Pima and Papago society was multifaceted. Masked dances similar to those of the Pueblos were held, but after the arrival of Europeans, these were reorganized to take place on the Spanish feast days and in honor of the Saints. It made a curious mix, in which age-old traditions of the Hohokams are blended with beliefs that originated in Mexico, from other tribes of the Southwest, and from Europe. When Apache tribes migrated from the north, resulting in conflict and intermittent warfare, the Pima and Papago accepted some Apache into their midst and took over new ideas from them.

THE APACHE

The slow migration of the Apache to the Southwest, which had taken over 500 years, was nearing completion at the time of the Spanish arrival. Perhaps the best known of the Apache tribes are the Jicarilla, Mescalero, and Chiricahua, but there were also dozens of small, independent groups, all speaking dialects of the Athapascan language. They brought with them a set of beliefs very different from those of the Pueblos or of the Pima and Papago. These beliefs originated in the northern forests of the Apache's Canadian homeland, where farming was impossible and the people were dependent on the proceeds of the hunt. The Apache lifestyle did not have the slow, repetitive cycles of the agriculturalists; hunting demanded a very different approach, in which long periods of waiting were rewarded in a few moments of extreme activity. Furthermore, because hunting was often a lone activity, the Apache valued individuality and personal decision more highly than did the Pueblo groups, among whom every act was intended to reinforce the cohesion of the tribe.

No member of an Apache band was formally bound by anything other than personal choice. This does not deny the solidarity of their clans, nor the influences exerted by having close relatives within the group or of speaking a particular dialect of the Apache language. Nevertheless, this lack of formal binding

Western Apache saddle bag, 1880. After horses had been introduced to the southern Plains by the Spanish, many Apache groups became equestrian, adapting the products they made to suit a mounted life. The large saddle bag shown here employs cut out rawhide over red and black cloth to create pattern.

Apache storage basket, nineteenth century. Apache tribes traded regularly with the Pueblos, exchanging products of the hunt for those of the fields. Grains obtained in trade were kept in large storage baskets, such as that depicted here, which could be as much as four feet high.

prevented the formation of highly organized tribal structures. People were free to follow the leader they chose, with the consequence that Apache bands were small and mobile, composed of people with a strong sense of independence and individual freedom.

The hunting economy of the Apache dictated that they remain nomadic, following the migrations of the animals on which they depended; it also introduced an element of aggressive response. This was apparent in their contacts with the Spanish, who brought horse herds into Santa Fe. The Apache raided the herds and became among the first of the American Indian tribes to acquire horses, enabling them to expand their hunting territories. This expansion led to the introduction of influences from tribal groups on the periphery of the Southwest area.

The Apache were a progressive people who readily adopted new trends and incorporated them into their cultural outlook. Apache clothing, for instance, was often made of deerskin and decorated with long fringe that is more readily associated with tribes of the Plains. Some groups, such as the Jicarilla and Kiowa-Apache, adopted the tepee as a dwelling instead of the traditional brush-covered wickiup. Yet at the same time they produced their own superbly executed basketwork, easily comparable in quality with that of the Pima and Papago. It included large carrying and storage baskets in which they kept grain.

Apache Gan dancers. Gans, or Mountain Spirits, are Apache spirits who returned to the people to confer blessings. When they returned, dancers impersonating them were characteristic costumes. The head-dresses contained symbols that were associated with the precipitation of water, a vital life-force in the arid Southwestern deserts.

APACHE MYTHOLOGY

Although the desert environments of the Southwest are very different from those of their original forests, the Apache quickly adapted and added new elements to an already rich mythology. It tells of their search for a homeland in which they were helped by the Twin War Gods, who traveled the earth and destroyed the monsters, thereby setting the world's boundaries and establishing areas in which the people could flourish. These are tales of a fantastic journey, assisted by Spider Woman and the other deities, which are merged with a colorful and lively view of an often difficult reality; tales of Changing Woman who, through continual renewal, change, and rejuvenation, is a dominant deity who symbolizes the essence of Apache thinking.

For the Apache, the world was in constant movement. There was no desire to bring it to a static center, and much of their ritual and belief focused on elements that were immediate and spontaneous. When an Apache "sang for horses" and told of the Sun String Bridle, he sang not to acquire but to celebrate; he told of the power invested in the bridle by the Sun, but placed there by himself through his own recognition of and participation in the release of Sun's energy. His horse was part of the land: its breath the air of the desert, its fleetness that of the wind. To the Apache, it was the same air, the same wind, that formed the people and the mesas; the same power warmed a sand grain and gave energy to the people.

Even their principal deities, the Gans or Mountain Spirits, have an immediacy that is quite different from anything possessed by other deities of the region (although most students of the Southwest place the origin of the Apache spirits firmly among the Pueblo). The strength of the Gans derives as much from the forest as the desert, and goes back to the Bear and Snake as surely as it links with Lightning and the Stars. But they are just as securely a part of the Southwest as the Kachinas, stemming from the suddenness of the land and nomadic needs rather than from a desire to create the constant, uniform patterns that are essential to agriculturalists.

THE DANCES OF THE GANS

The Mountain Spirits dance only at night, before huge fires that throw them constantly from illumination into shadow. When they appear, there is a hushed awareness of the awesome power they possess. Their dance is a searching one, and they come from the Four Directions, approaching the fire from east, south, west, and north. They utter cries that echo back to the past and have a primeval simplicity and directness that reaches an unconscious chord deep within one's own recognition.

Through the performance, the people relive the origin of the Apache and the migrations of their ancestors. The blessings the Mountain Spirits confer are passed through the women of the tribe, who enclose the spirits in a slowly moving circle that is danced at the rim of the firelight. There are reminders, however, that the Mountain Spirits are not all-powerful. A clown accompanies them. Following behind, he shakes rattles and mimicks their movements in a humorous and grotesque manner. But he is the most sacred of the dancers, who guards the Mountain Spirits and turns away negative influences by preventing them from entering the circle.

The juxtaposition of seriousness and humor characterizes much of Apache life, and visitors to their ceremonies are frequently surprised, and sometimes shocked, to find rituals of a deeply religious nature taking place alongside social dances, gambling, and horse racing. But the contradiction is in the mind of the visitor, who has failed to see that the need to celebrate and rejoice is as sacred to the Apache as is the mumbled chant of a shaman (or medicine man) while sprinkling colored earth to make a holy sandpainting. The celebrations are an affirmation of life and not disrespect for the rituals.

Apache cap, nineteenth century. This cap of white deerskin is decorated with paint and owl feathers. Whether it was worn by a girl at puberty ceremonies or by a warrior is unclear, but the painted decoration is linked with the Lightning Snake, the Stars, and the Sky, and ties the symbolism of the cap to the life-giving powers of the Gans.

THE NAVAJO

Of the many Apache bands, one requires separate mention because it forged an identity unlike that of other Apache groups. They were originally only a small band, named by the Spanish as the Apaches de Nabaju because they were first seen in the vicinity of an abandoned Pueblo village of that name. They are now the largest North American Indian tribe and have a reservation that is half the size of England. These are the Navajo. They, too, assimilated new ideas, which were blended with their own beliefs and material expressions to create artforms that are uniquely theirs. The Navajo blanket, with its bold colors and patterns, is perhaps their best-known artifact and could not be confused with the blankets and weavings of any other tribe. Yet weaving was a skill learned from the Pueblos, and the wool came from sheep that had been introduced into the area by the Spanish. The uniqueness of the blankets arises from the fact that the Navajo beliefs expressed in the designs stem from an ancient origin outside the Southwest area, but are also dependent on the nature of the desert.

Navajo families adopted a different lifestyle from that of other Apaches. Many of the basic structures, such as extended family groupings and clans rather than tribal affiliations, remained. But their flocks of sheep turned them from being primarily hunters into herders, although the proceeds from hunting were still important. They began to plant orchards of peach trees on the flat bottomlands of the magnificent Canyon de Chelly and had some limited farming of other crops.

Navajo sun string silver bridle, *c* 1870. The Navajo used precious metals to adorn bridles from the time of their first contacts with the Spanish, obtaining both horses and silver by trading. It was not until 1850, however, that silversmithing was learned from the Mexicans. By 1870, a distinctive Indian style had emerged.

Navajo serape, 1860. This Moki-style serape contains a mixture of hand-spun and revelled yarns. The background is woven in natural brown and indigo blue stripes, on which are terraced diamonds of carded and ravelled bayeta yarns. Although woven by women, they were always worn by men.

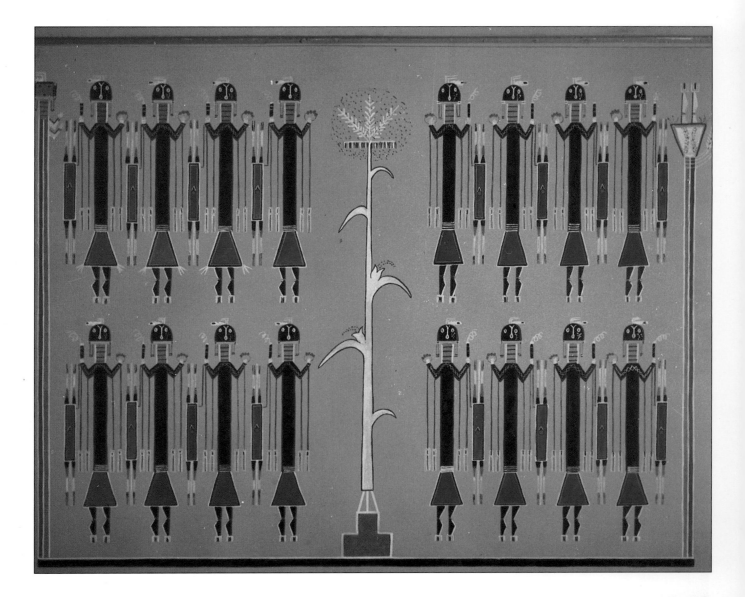

Despite these changes, the Navajo remained an essentially nomadic people. Their octagonal pole and brush shelters, or hogans, were scattered so widely that any contacts between families involved lengthy journeys. Even so, they maintained close communities and visited other hogans regularly, uniquely combining the need of the herder and farmer to stay close to the flocks and fields with that of the nomad to travel. One may still today come across a Navajo striding purposefully toward some distant goal through a country that shows no sign of visible habitation.

The principal deities of the Navajo, the Yeis, although having much in common with the Kachinas and Gans as ancestral forces that generally lived apart from the people, are defined in other ways. They are represented in a special category of blanket, the Yei blanket, where they are often shown surrounded by the rainbow. The Yeis appear among the people only on the eighth day of a lengthy healing chant known as the Night Way, or Yeibichai. They then instruct children in the mysteries of the spirit world. At the end of the performance, they remove their masks, revealing that they are, after all, human and that the worlds of people and the spirits do not simply coexist, but are ultimately the same.

Sandpainting, Navajo. This sandpainting from the Navajo Yeibichai, or Night Way Chant, depicts the Sixteen Black Fire Gods. Shamans made sandpaintings from colored earths and cornmeal to form an "altar" as part of elaborate curing rituals.

Navajo weaver, c1890. Navajo weaving was on an upright loom that could be erected or dismantled quickly and easily.

Navajo dress, 1880. Although Navajo blankets were worn by men, the same weaving techniques were used to produce dresses for women. The two-piece dress shown here is a magnificient example and illustrates the strong graphic sense for which Navajo weavers are well known.

Blanket, Navajo.

Squash-blossom necklace, Navajo, early twentieth century. With the development of distinctive styles of silver working after 1870, generic groups of jewelry emerged. One of these was the "squash-blossom necklace", so-named for the bell-shaped attachments on the necklace string.

San Ildefonso platter, c1925. A rare example of the pottery of Maria and Julian Martinez. In the early 1920s, the Martinezes attempted to recreate the blackware pottery of the San Ildefonso Pueblo, which was then known only from archaeological fragments. This platter is one of the first examples of a pottery style for which San Aldofonso is famous today.

Silver and turquoise ring, Navajo, c1930. By the 1920s, the Navajo were using semi-precious stones in their silver jewelry. Turquoise was a favorite. In early examples, the stone is uncut and its shape is incorporated into the design, as in this superb ring, which has a single nugget of turquoise nearly 1½ inches in length.

THE FORCES OF THE LAND

All the peoples of the Southwest, although their life-styles and beliefs differed widely, felt that they lived within the land rather than simply on it. As natural parts of the living environment they express, through their myths, rituals, and art, the forces that are contained in the land. Power – in the Indian sense of a personal and collective consciousness – comes from an understanding and recognition of these forces. It is invested in the pattern and weave of baskets and blankets, and in the paintings on pottery. It is the same power that is ritually concentrated and directed through the medium of sandpaintings. These are made as part of a long series of chants of tremendous complexity, during which energy is focused as an aid in the restoration of harmony. None of these material or ritual manifestations can truly be separated from the collective understanding of the people who produce them; neither can they be parted from the environment by which they are inspired.

Silver earrings, Hopi. The work of Navajo silversmiths influenced other groups of the Southwest, who developed characteristic techniques. Hopi craftsmen employed a "layering" method in which a thin sheet of silver was oxidized to turn it black and then fastened beneath a second sheet bearing cut-out designs.

Group of Southwestern bracelets. The bracelets shown here vary in date from very early examples to one that was made in 1990. They illustrate the stability and continuity that was so much a part of Southwestern life. This stability has enabled the groups to retain much of their tradition.

CHAPTER TWO

The Far North

Icy Cape Eskimo men with labrets, Alaska, c1880. The Eskimo placed an emphasis on individual status. Among the western groups, high ranking boys had their lower lip pierced at puberty and a small wooden or ivory plug inserted. The size of this plug, or labret, was increased as they aged and gained further standing.

THE ESKIMO

THE EXTREME NORTH APPEARS incapable of supporting life. Its vistas are great expanses of snow. The landscape shifts as Arctic winds catch the surface snow and scatter it in dense, impenetrable blizzards, creating a white wall that conceals what lies behind it. When the winds subside and vision is restored, mountainous snow banks that seemed permanent have disappeared, while new ones have replaced them in unfamiliar locations. Vision is further restricted by the winter night – for nearly six months the sun never rises. In summer, the sun refuses to set, although the summer season is short and lasts a mere six weeks. Conceptions of space and time are dramatically different here. This land of impermanence and bitter cold is home to the Eskimo-Aleut, a people living on the edge of the habitable world. The Eskimo and Aleut shared a common cultural heritage and spoke dialects of the same language, but separated in the distant past. The Aleut lived on the Aleutian Islands, whereas the Eskimo, speaking a number of dialects, were spread from Asia across the north of the American continent and into Greenland.

Eskimo life exists firmly in the present. Their constantly changing environment leaves no icons to its past, nor any focus that can be returned to. The land has no discernible history, and there is little point in looking back because there is no fixity to look back to. Its future is uncertain and can never be a logical progression from the present because the present is continually being redefined. In such a world, the rituals, tales, and legends must concentrate on recent and current events. Although the Eskimo were nomadic, they did not have the ancestral migration tales typical of most nomads. Elaborate burials are likewise absent, for there is little reason to ceremonially inter the dead if the place of burial will soon cease to exist. Similarly, it was futile to prepare for a future that might never arrive.

The line between life and death is narrow in the Arctic. The environment permits no half-measures and results in certain Eskimo customs that have an uncompromising harshness. The sick or the elderly might be left exposed on the ice if they were too weak

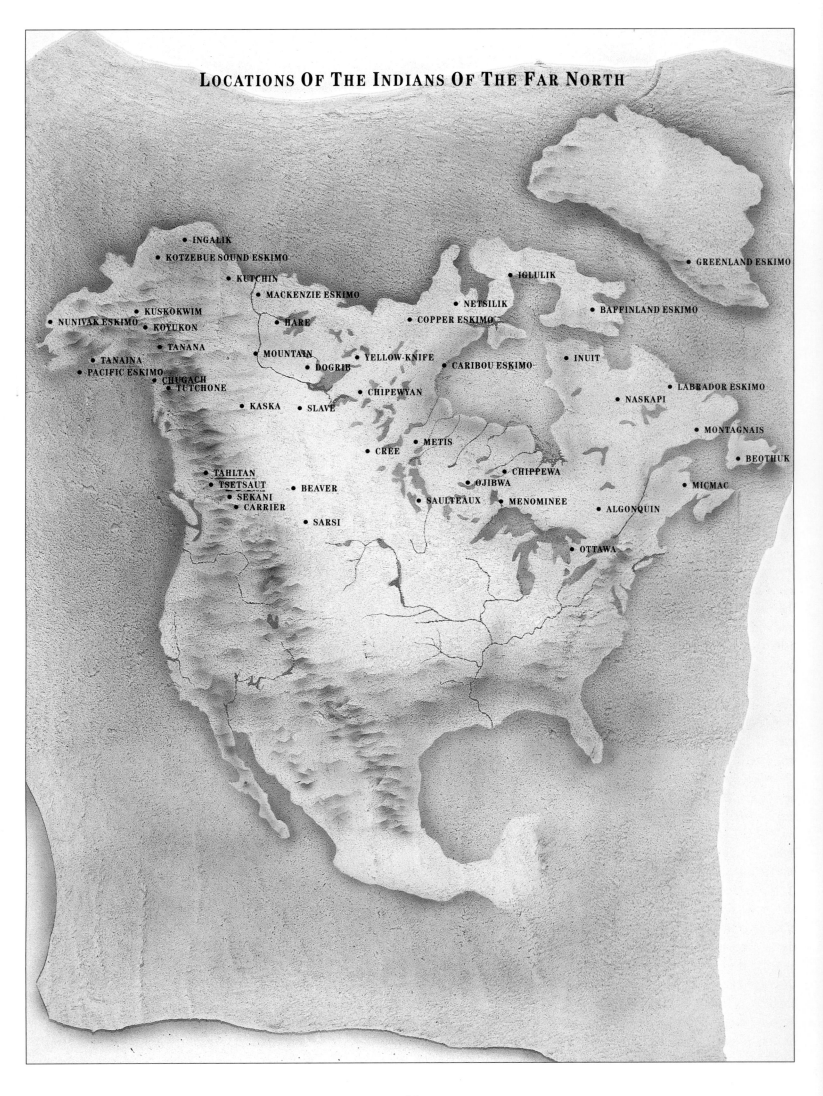

LOCATIONS OF THE INDIANS OF THE FAR NORTH

- INGALIK
- KOTZEBUE SOUND ESKIMO
- GREENLAND ESKIMO
- KUTCHIN
- IGLULIK
- MACKENZIE ESKIMO
- KUSKOKWIM
- NETSILIK
- BAFFINLAND ESKIMO
- NUNIVAK ESKIMO
- KOYUKON
- HARE
- COPPER ESKIMO
- TANANA
- MOUNTAIN
- YELLOW-KNIFE
- INUIT
- TANAINA
- DOGRIB
- CARIBOU ESKIMO
- PACIFIC ESKIMO
- CHUGACH
- LABRADOR ESKIMO
- TUTCHONE
- CHIPEWYAN
- NASKAPI
- KASKA
- SLAVE
- MONTAGNAIS
- METIS
- BEOTHUK
- CREE
- TAHLTAN
- CHIPPEWA
- TSETSAUT
- OJIBWA
- MICMAC
- SEKANI
- BEAVER
- SAULTEAUX
- MENOMINEE
- ALGONQUIN
- CARRIER
- SARSI
- OTTAWA

to keep up with the group; death would come quickly in this hostile environment. Outsiders see cruelty in these practices, yet the Eskimo were close families. Their environment, however, demanded instant responses. Mobility was of paramount importance, and a slight slowing of their speed of travel during attempts to avoid harsh weather or reach food sources could mean the entire band would perish. The sacrifice of the weak was a deep personal loss to every member of the community, but it was dictated by necessity and carried out from communal need.

In so bleak and rigorous a land, we might expect the people to adopt a determined but resigned outlook. Instead, the Eskimo used laughter and humor as antidotes to severity. Reports of visitors to their camps stress their jovial character and that singing, playing games and practical joking were constant activities. In many ways, the extreme precariousness of living in the Arctic heightened their sense of the preciousness of life. Laughter and singing were expressions of this, and cheerfulness was a major aid to survival because it created a sense of hope.

WELCOMING WINTER

The Eskimo were not, however, completely governed by the dictates of their environment. Although maintaining flexibility on a day-to-day basis was essential and long-term planning of relatively little importance, they were nevertheless highly practical, adaptive, and inventive. They were able to turn the extremes of their habitat to advantage. Among the independent inventions of the Eskimo are snow goggles, barbed fishing spears, toggle harpoons, dog sleds, kayaks, and igloos. Among the western groups, the onset of colder winter weather was welcomed because it made life easier. For instance, sled runners, washed over with water that froze instantly, ran smoothly over firm snow; travel was faster than in summer, when thaws created treacherous patches of thin ice.

In the central area of the far north, the snow house, or igloo, was used as a winter dwelling – another instance of the cold being employed advantageously. By closing the entrance of a newly erected igloo and lighting a seal-oil lamp, the joins between the snow blocks from which it was constructed began to thaw. If the entrance was then opened, the inrush of cold air froze the joins and welded them into a solid wall of ice. Slightly higher summer temperatures disturbed the equilibrium between the warmth inside the igloo and the cold outside, making the dwelling damp. At this time, the people moved closer to the shorelines, abandoning the igloos that might be several miles out on now-dangerous sea ice. They erected sod shelters or used sealskin-covered lodges similar to those used in other parts of the Eskimo area.

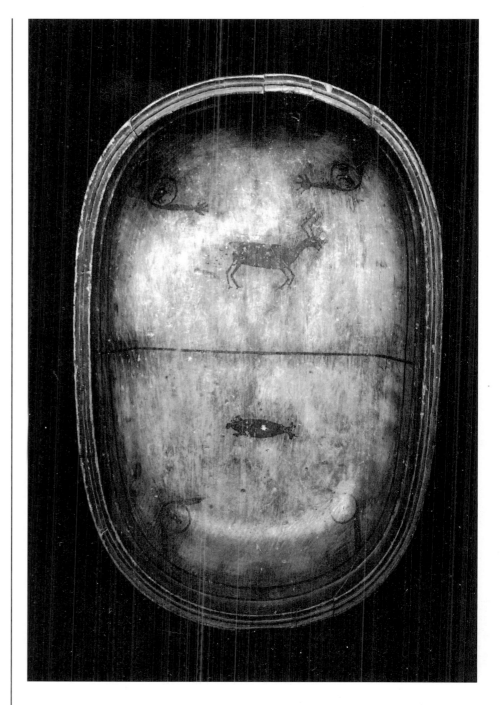

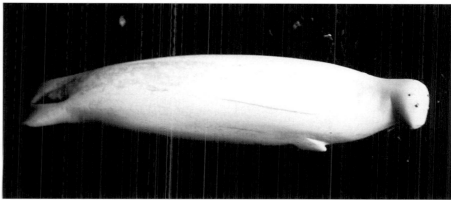

▲ ▲ Wooden bowl, Eskimo, Kuskokwim River, Alaska, c1920. Carved from a single piece of spruce, this bowl depicts the summer and winter activities of the Kuskokwim River Eskimo. One half shows a caribou to represent the summer hunting season; the other half contains the image of a walrus, the principal winter quarry. The bowl is exceptionally large.

▲ Ivory seal charm, Eskimo, Bering Sea/High Arctic. Eskimo carvers were highly skilled, and their work demonstrates an acute understanding of animals and animal behaviour.

PROTECTION FROM THE COLD

Although the temperatures of the High Arctic seem unbelievably bitter to people accustomed to warmer climates, cold was never a matter of serious concern to the Eskimo. Body warmth could be maintained by several layers of light clothing that trapped warm air. Seal-oil lamps gave off sufficient heat to keep dwellings adequately comfortable. Far greater problems were wind and rain. If clothing became wet, body warmth would rapidly be lost, resulting in hypothermia or severe frostbite. Clothing was therefore designed specifically to keep warmth in and wind and water out. Lightweight seal-gut parkas, often richly decorated with linear patterns of fiber and feathers, were totally wind- and waterproof. Fur trimmings on the parka hoods kept wind away from the face, preventing condensed breath from freezing. Boots of sealskin or heavier caribou skin had seams sewn on the inside so as not to let water enter.

Weatherproof clothing was essential to a hunter who spent hours standing motionless at a seal breathing hole. He could not afford to be numbed by the cold and had to stay alert, ready to thrust his spear accurately as soon as a seal appeared. A misplaced strike, resulting in a wounding rather than a kill, could allow the seal to escape beneath the ice. There would be no possibility of pursuit, and it might be several days before another chance presented itself. Summer hunting was easier. Seals basking on offshore ice floes could be harpooned from fast sealing canoes, or kayaks. Sea mammals, such as walruses, too big to hunt from easily capsized kayaks, were pursued in larger umiaks capable of carrying from 10 to 12 men.

The resources that the Eskimo depended on were generally scarce, however, and this resulted in communal sharing. Food was owned equally by all members of a group, and the situation never arose in which one person had plenty and another went without. Excesses were stored in caches dug in the snow in sheltered places, where they would freeze and stay edible for several years. Although many of the caches were lost under drifting snow, those that were recoverable were available to any traveler.

GREAT FEASTS

Such sharing is indicative of the fact that the Eskimo are a big-hearted, generous people with a strong need for constant friendship and companionship. The Arctic, however, provides too little to support large populations, so the typical Eskimo band was a small group who were closely related by blood or through marriage. The focus of their life was the family, but in the summer several families might come together for celebrations that could continue unabated for days at a time. Great feasts were held, and gambling, singing, dancing, and contests of skill were carried out in an atmosphere of sensual intimacy. The abandon was such that early travelers described them as people with little foresight and fewer morals, whose only concern was the immediate gratification of their various passions and desires.

PRUDENCE AND CAUTION

Such descriptions accurately portray the feast gatherings, but these were rare events that celebrated a temporary release from the need to be prudent. The Eskimo were acutely aware that, although the feast could last for a week or more, they would then scatter widely, and it was very possible that for several months they might have contact only with the members of their own family band. If passions and desires were

▼ ▬▬▬▬▬▬▬▬
Seal or walrus gut parkas, mittens, and bag, Aleut, Yukon and Bering Strait area, _c_ 1880. Seal and walrus gut were valued for the manufacture of clothing and storage bags in the Western Arctic areas. Items made from these were lightweight and offered absolute protection against wind and water.

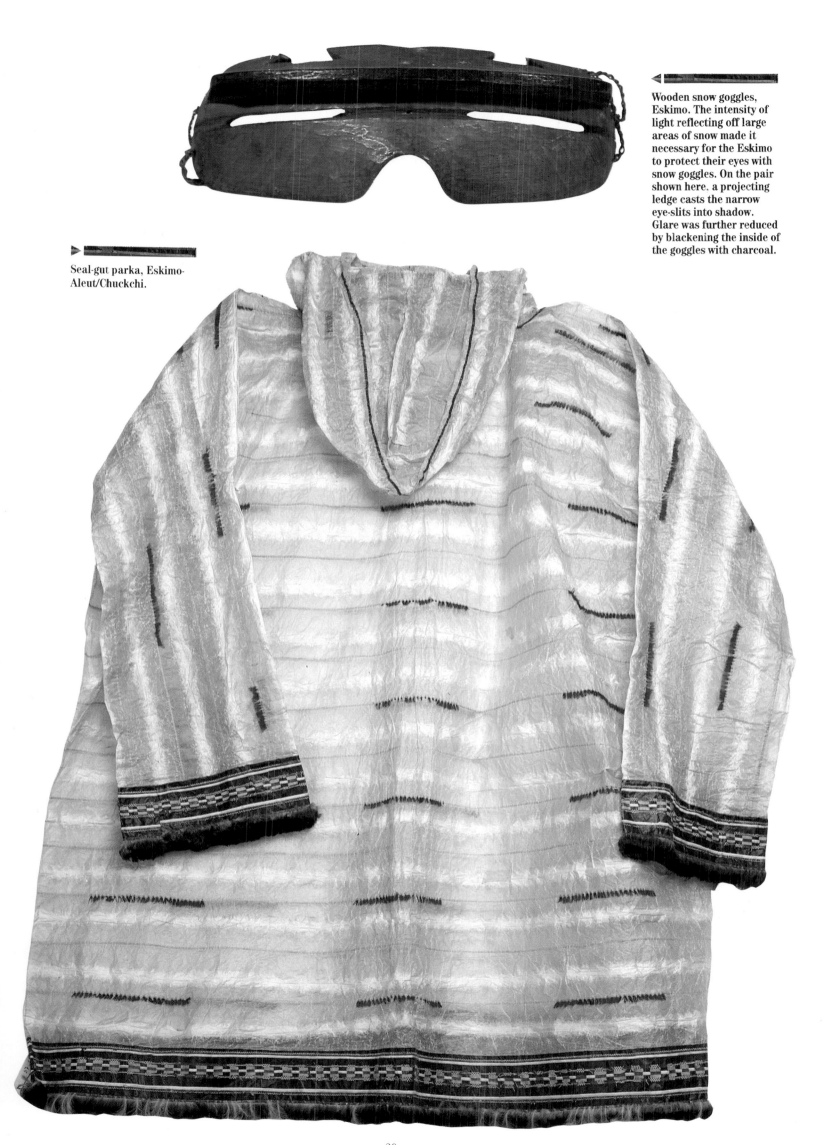

Wooden snow goggles, Eskimo. The intensity of light reflecting off large areas of snow made it necessary for the Eskimo to protect their eyes with snow goggles. On the pair shown here, a projecting ledge casts the narrow eye-slits into shadow. Glare was further reduced by blackening the inside of the goggles with charcoal.

Seal-gut parka, Eskimo-Aleut/Chuckchi.

not expressed openly and urgently at the feasts, they could not be expressed at all.

For the rest of the year, every action was marked by caution, and each member of the community listened carefully for warning sounds carried by the winds and paid attention to the predictions of the shamans, or *angakoks,* because the guidance they could offer stemmed from the advice of powerful unseen spirits. Not all the predictions came true, but the shaman – their senses highly attuned to the signs and sounds around them – were accurate often enough for their predictions to be taken seriously.

SPIRITS AND SHAMANS

The character of the spirits the shamans contacted was determined by the nature of snow blizzards, when only vague shapes, created by varying densitites in the driven snow, can be discerned. These gave indeterminate form to spirits that hovered just out of sight and were open to individual interpretation. They were fearsome creatures whose nature derived from the ice, cold, sleet, and bitter chill of the land. A shaman was protected by his or her supernatural power.

Some spirits were recognized widely and began to gain status as major deities. Among these are Air and Moon, which may be combined on a mask with feathers representing stars and rings signifying the levels of the cosmos. But none of the spirits had the universality of Sedna, the Sea Mother, the immortal child of giant parents who abandoned her at sea when they could no longer satisfy her voracious appetite. From her underwater realm, she controls the movements and migrations of the fishes and sea mammals. Sedna is easily angered and can whip up terrifying storms. She is a formidable force, possessing a power that can crack icebergs. Only the most powerful shamans would ever seek to converse with her during supernatural journeys beneath the seas, when they spoke in the ancient language of the Eskimo that only they understood.

For the most part, however, the Eskimo came to terms with the spirit forces in the same way as they dealt with other facets of their lives: through humor. Driftwood masks of even the most dangerous supernaturals often have a comic appearance. The Eskimo did not exhibit a fear of the spirits, accepting them as matter-of-fact elements of their country, but were cautious in their dealings with them and adept in keeping them at a distance. Small ivory charms, traditionally worn as necklaces or sewn into clothing, helped to dispel negative influences. The charms frequently have one or two bright blue beads, the color of the Arctic seas, that represent the breath of life and through which the charm becomes animated.

Not all charms were used in this way. Many were

Sun visor, Aleut, mid nineteenth century. The Aleut and southwest Alaskan Eskimos wore bentwood sun visors when hunting from kayaks. This example is decorated with cormorant feathers, and has ivory carvings that indicate the wearer's high rank and are intended to influence seals and walrus to ensure the success of the hunt.

made with the intention of releasing a benign animal spirit considered trapped within the confines of a piece of ivory or bone. The carver listened carefully to the sounds of the wind passing over the contours of the ivory until eventually the nature of the spirit was revealed. Then, with a minimum number of cuts, he would release the spirit by carving its image. Such charms may be delicate representations of seals rising to the surface to breathe, or of polar bears engaged in a wrestling match, and are executed with obvious care and attention to detail. But once their function was served, they might be discarded. They are a fitting tribute to the immediacy of Eskimo life; to the necessity of performing an action swiftly and precisely, but then moving on directly to other activities.

THE TUNDRA

Along the southern fringes of the Eskimo homeland, the ice and snow give way to tundra. Stretching across the northern third of Canada, the tundra is marked by a layer of permanently frozen subsoil, or permafrost, only a few inches (centimeters) below the surface. Thaws in the summer create a marshy swampland in which grasses, sedges, and lichens can take root. At this time the area attracts a phenomenal number of migratory birds and great herds of caribou. Eskimos hunted regularly here, where they came in contact with Athapascan- and Algonquian-speaking Indians from the subarctic forests that cover much of the rest of Canada and parts of Alaska.

Auk skin coat, Aleut, Kodiak Island. An early example of bird-skin clothing from Kodiak Island. It is made from the skins of the great auk and is decorated with auk beaks, trade-cloth, and twisted thread to which is attached tufts of downy feathers. It is nearly 2 meters wide, and was worn by a man of high status.

Wooden Ladle, Ingalik. This ladle is similar in form to ladies made by Athapascan groups, such as the Tanaina, although the red and black lines indicate that it is more likely to be Ingalik. Wooden items of this type were traded widely; and were treasured items that would be placed on the grave of the owner.

Chagamiuts (Chugach), Yupik Eskimo. The Chagamiut, or Chugach, lived between various cultural areas, and they exhibit a bewildering array of culture traits. For example, the man here wears a basketwork hat that is very similar to those of the Northwest Coast Nootka, but also has what appears to be a hooded gut-parka of Eskimo type.

Ivory Otterman charm, Chugach. This early ivory carving depicts the Otterman, a highly feared supernatural who exercised tremendous shamanic influence. The Otterman is generally associated with the peoples of the Northwest Coast, but the style of this carving suggests it is from the Chugach, who lived on Prince William Sound.

THE ATHAPASCAN

Athapascan, from an Algonquian-Cree word meaning "strangers," is a linguistic classification used when referring to a number of small tribes who spoke related languages and knew themselves by derivatives of Dene or Tine, "The People." Their territories lay to the west of Hudson Bay. Along the western shore of the Bay and reaching a considerable distance into the interior were the lands of the Chipewyan, the largest of the Dene group. In the central part of the area lived the Kaska, Mountain, Beaver, Slavey, Bear Lake, Dogrib, and Yellowknife. Further west, closer to the eastern slopes of the Rocky Mountains, were the Atna, Tutchone, Tahltan, Carrier, and Chilcotin. The Koyukon, Ingalik, Tanana, and Kutchin lived in the Yukon and Mackenzie River valleys and drainages in Alaska. The most southerly of the northern Athapascan were the Sarsi, a small group in Alberta who had allied themselves with the Blackfoot of the Plains and adopted a nomadic, buffalo-hunting culture.

Quiver, probably Tanaina. The painted figures, hunters and animals, the only mysterious animal being the "bug-like" creature at the top centre of the quiver. There is reason to think that this is a "mythical beast", painted to imbue the contents of the quiver with magical properties.

Kutchin woman. The woman in this picture was drawn by John Webber during Captain James Cook's third voyage (1776–79). Her facepaint shows a vertical line comparable with that on Kutchin and Tanaina clothing. The beaded yoke of her dress shows traditional form and cut.

Dress, Kutchin, pre 1850.
Mittens, Kutchin, 1862.
Dress and leggings, Cook
Inlet, Tanaina, pre 1850.
Members of leading
families among the
Northern Athapascan,

Tanaina and Kutchin wore
matching costumes of a
dress or tunic, leggings
which generally had
attached mocassins,
sheathed knife, mittens,
and sometimes a hood.

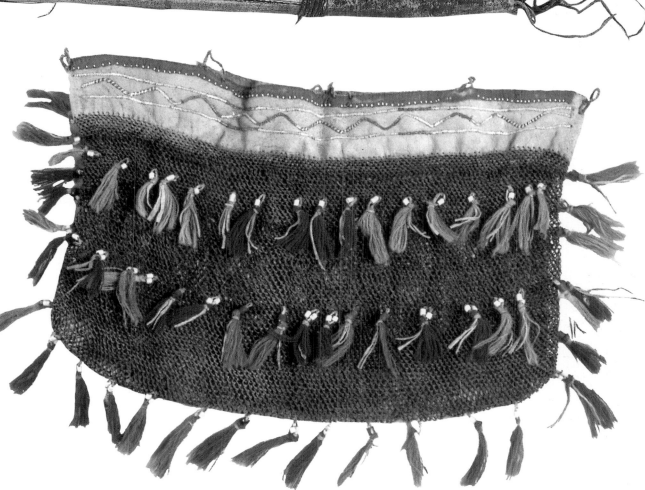

Caribou-antler club, Tanaina. Collected near the Kenai Peninsula, which means it is almost certainly Tanaina, this club has shell and turquoise inserts along its side. A photograph cannot convey the size and weight of the club: it is very large and heavy. A small obsidian blade was possibly inset into the club, but this has been lost.

Hunting bag of netted babiche, Hare, 1860. The northern Athapascan tribes used netted bags made from babiche – a thin rawhide rope cut in a spiral from a single piece of hide. The bag shown here has a tanned caribou-skin opening and is decorated with bands of pigment, wool, bead dangles, and goose quills.

The country of the Dene was one where the wind met resistance from the trees and so was reduced and quieted. It is an enclosed habitat, particularly in the dense forests in the southern part of the area where innumerable streams twist along dark passageways overhung with vegetation. Vision is restricted, but it is a very different restriction from that of the Arctic. Trees interrupt sight rather than snow storms forbidding it; there were always visible indicators of the forces that operated here. All these forces were nearby and were expressed with a quiet beauty.

Every element in the Dene homeland was subdued. In these northern forests, the sun filters rather than blazes, and the transition from light to shadow is always veiled and indistinct. It is a land that seems to imply rather than assert, and because of this the art-forms of the area are introverted. Power, instead of being released into an indefinable void as in Eskimo carving, is concentrated and focused in the object itself. The intricacies of delicate porcupine quillwork and moosehair embroidery need to be held in the hand and kept close; the detail and subtlety are contemplated rather than being suddenly realized.

DREAMS AND DREAMING

Such qualities characterize Dene thinking and are demonstrated through dreams and visions that direct the life of every individual. These are never overt power-dreams giving control of spirit forces, but are everyday dreams in which clues and hints may be discovered. They stem from a landscape in which minor detail may reveal a greater whole. A hunter examining the tracks of an animal knew not only its species, but also the direction and speed of its travel,

Bear tooth charm, Athapascan, nineteenth century. The Bear was a symbol of physical and supernatural power throughout the Athapascan area, and possession of a charm that linked the owner with the Bear was considered to be particularly beneficial. This example has fine porcupine quillwork decoration.

Bark-scraper, Carrier Indians, Moricetown, pre 1925. This bark-scraper has characteristic dot and circle patterns that were widespread in the far north. It is made from caribou antler. Scrapers of this type were used to remove sap from the inner layer of jack-pine bark to be used as food.

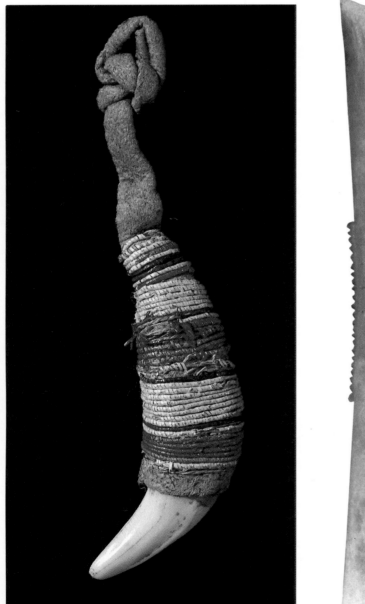

Hood, probably Tanaina. This hood is made from buckskin and embellished with bird skin, porcupine quills, beads, red pigment, and fiber. The hood would have been worn as part of a complete costume.

Mittens, Tanaina.

the approximate age of the animal, and even its gender. From such clues the hunter could predict what the animal would do next. But the success of the hunt was inextricably bound to dreams, and often an animal would first be hunted down through a dream; the success of the dream hunt meant that the hunter would secure the animal he sought.

Dreams were of essential importance in the forests which barely managed to hold back forces that created uncertainty and danger. Most of the malignant powers belonged to the realm of the unknown and the unexpected, but through dreams they might be recognized and understood, and appropriate action taken to minimize their threat. Such psychological advantage was critical in an area where resources can be limited and hard to obtain. It could only operate at an individual level, however, and the rituals and taboos associated with it were always expressed as intensely personal beliefs, which emphasized the individuality inherent in Dene households.

In this world of constant threat, shamanism reached a high level of development. Both men and women might be shamans, or Dreamers, who occasionally inherited their power, but more often received it involuntarily while they slept. In essence, a shaman's power was no different from the personal aids sought by others. The Dreamers were simply considered to be more receptive and to have extraordinary sensitivity, so much so that they could communicate with each other over vast distances with their dream-messages and could pool their resources without the need to come into any physical proximity. In many ways, shamans transcended their environment, because here, where travel was never easy, the dream enabled thoughts to be projected to infinity.

CAMPS AND VILLAGES

Although the groups traveled fairly extensively, they did so within well-defined boundaries, utilizing established villages and campsites that were returned to regularly. Spring and early summer were spent in

temporary camps near muskrat lodges, where berries could be gathered and birchbark collected for repairing containers and to provide materials for canoes and housing. Summer camps were also erected at weirs on fish-bearing rivers; fall camps were near the trap-lines and close to deer or caribou routes; winter was spent in sheltered areas that offered some protection from the intense cold of the region and where permanent villages were sited. Villages in the western part of the Dene area consisted of log cabins, whereas in the east they used birchbark lodges.

Alexander Mackenzie, the first European to visit the Dene camps of southern British Columbia, commented on the plank houses he found here. He noted that many had elaborately carved roof-support beams, and that the villages were located in clearings along the edges of lakes. Nearby were small huts in which the bones of the deceased were placed and which were obviously subject to continual care – the ground around them was well tended and kept free of growth.

All these camps were small, inhabited at most by about thirty or fifty people in the more favorable areas and by fewer in some parts of the north. Those who lived in the camps had an extraordinary sensitivity for the land, knew the local country absolutely, and were aware of the numbers of any animal species within a distance of several miles. Many resources were scattered, although they could be seasonally plentiful in specific localities. Hunters traveled widely in pursuit of game, relying on the superior sense of their dogs to locate animals and to retrace their path to the village.

The regularly occupied campsites provided a degree of stability, but security could only be provided through the performance of ritual acts intended to avert danger. Family heads knew ways of calming forces that could disrupt village life by following taboos and other observations; hunters were careful to honor the animals they killed and not to take life unnecessarily. Most ritual, in fact, consisted of understated acts intended to show respect, such as placing small items of food near a place where one's animal spirit-familiar resided, or visiting such a place and pausing there in concentrated thought.

Such deep reverence is clearly an environmental response, reflecting the unhurried subtlety of the northern forests. It is found in all Dene activities. Nothing took place without prior consultation and careful planning, although this might be accomplished in such a quiet manner that someone unacquainted with their life would have noticed nothing. White visitors in Dene households have been frequently surprised when a unanimous decision about a particular course of action has been announced, since they were unaware that anything was even under consideration.

THE ALGONQUIN

The hunting and gathering lifestyle of the Athapascan was shared by the Algonquian-speaking tribes of the eastern Subarctic. The environment, climatic conditions, and animal species in the region are, in essence, the same as those of the Dene lands. The principal tribe was the Cree, with numerous small bands scattered over a huge area abutting the Dene lands and reaching beyond the Great Lakes to the east, and south into the Prairie provinces of Canada. Some of the more southerly Cree bands became equestrian and moved onto the northern fringes of the Plains. Here they were joined by some Ojibwa, a subarctic off-shoot of the Chippewa tribes of the Eastern Woodlands. Further east were the Algonquin – a small tribe who have given their name to the entire language group – and near the mouth of the St. Lawrence River and on Newfoundland were the Micmac, Beothuk, and Montagnais. North of these groups, in Labrador, were the Naskapi.

Algonquian groups are descendants of early hunters and farmers of the eastern forests who moved north with the retreat of the glaciers some 10,000 to 12,000 years ago. Farming was impossible in the Subarctic – with the exception of some small garden plots in the extreme south of the region – and all the tribes adopted hunting economies. Among the Cree, there was a strong reliance on small game and fur-bearing animals in the northern parts of their territory, with deer becoming the principal quarry in the south. The Ojibwa also hunted deer, but wild rice was another important part of their diet. The Micmac and Beothuk, although they hunted in the interior, were primarily sea fishermen. The Naskapi, who had to contend with the severe Labrador environment – the forests consist of sparse, dwarf trees, and the seas freeze in winter and carry icebergs in summer – were primarily caribou hunters. They used its skins to make fitted coats painted with elaborate decoration.

Knife sheath, Great Lakes area, Cree/Menominee. Decorated with zig-zag porcupine quillwork on its body, this buckskin sheath has checker-board quillwork on the strap. Tin cone dangles with dyed hair pendants hang beneath the opening to the sheath. Such sheaths were worn around the neck.

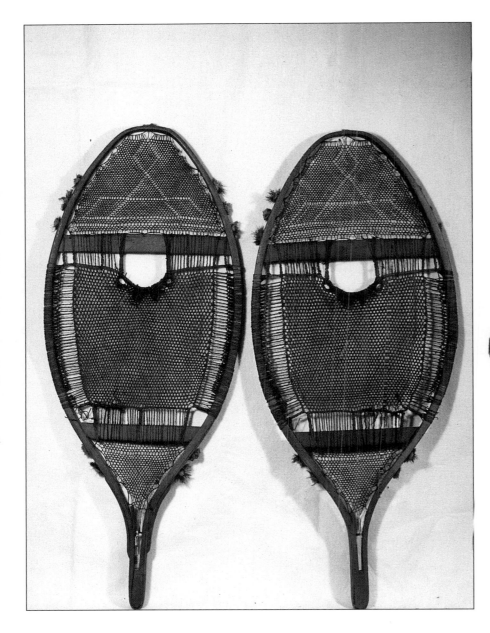

Snowshoes, Eskimo.

Nest of baskets, Cree, 1720–1745. These thirty birchbark baskets all fit perfectly together. They are made from the bark of White or Paper birch; both barks were valued for their tough, durable and weatherproof qualities. Birchbark was used throughout the Subarctic area for a variety of different purposes.

Quilled shot pouches, Cree/Ojibwa, Great Lakes area, nineteenth century. With the replacement of the bow and arrows by the gun, it became necessary to carry shot and powder. Powder was carried in carved and decorated horns. Shot was kept in a skin pouch decorated with porcupine quills, such as the examples here.

TOTEMIC DESCENT

Environmental fators determined the maximum size
of group that could be successfully maintained and
insured that most remained as small, loosely affiliated,
family bands. In the more temperate south, larger
groupings were possible, and the Ojibwa had some
settled villages; but the extreme conditions in Labrador

dictated that the basic Naskapi social unit consisted
simply of a husband and wife with their children, and
perhaps one or two elderly relatives.

The belief systems in the eastern Subarctic are
perhaps best exemplified by those of the Cree, because
strong Woodlands influence is apparent among other
tribes such as the Ojibwa. Among the Cree, the powers
of ancestors are the driving force. Every newborn
child was carefully examined for physical signs, such
as a mole or birthmark, that might demonstrate a
link with a particular deceased relative. If such a sign
was found, the child would be given that person's
name. This custom crossed gender barriers; thus, a
girl baby bearing a mark associated with a man would

▼ ▬▬▬▬▬▬▬

**Birchbark box decorated
with porcupine quills,
Micmac, mid nineteenth
century. The Micmac**
tribes of Newfoundland
were highly regarded for
their quilled birchbark
boxes. These were made
by women.

be given a male name, and her character would be
deemed influenced by him.

Through a system of totemic descent, each individual was also linked with the original animal spirits
and so to a distant mythological time before the people
and the animals separated. Each person was considered to have close ties with a specific animal
species. So definite is this that even the word "totem,"
used in its anthropological context, comes from the
Cree word *"ototema,"* meaning "one's relations".

The totemic link was considered particularly
beneficial to hunters. It is a very different concept to
that of animal-familiars. A person inspired by the
wolf, for example, did not see the animal as a guide
and helper that would offer assistance if treated with
respect, but as a distant relative under an obligation
to help. In summer, a hunter in a canoe could use a
birchbark moose call, and the animal would willingly
come to the bank of a river or lake where its movements would be hampered by marshy ground; in
winter, a moose would leave clear tracks so that a
man on snowshoes could follow it easily.

Ceremonies were performed in which the dancers
became the embodiment of the animals they represented; a status acknowledged in and defined by
the blood relationship said to exist between them.
This lent credence to the belief that bodily form was
transitory and, in the case of particularly potent
forces, could be changed at will. Thus the bear might
appear in the guise of a sturgeon in order to be able
to assist a human relative in the separate activities of
fishing and hunting.

COMMON ORIGINS

At a higher level, the cosmic elements were continually transforming themselves during heroic battles
that only the fittest could survive. The victors passed
on their knowledge through rituals that enabled the
people to deal with hardship and severe circum-
stances. On a lesser scale, the reborn hunter might
return as a deer or other animal, or even as a plant
or rock, because the Cree did not make a distinction
between animate and inanimate, considering everything to have one common ancestral origin.

The Cree conception of the relationship between
people, animals, and plants leads to a conceptualiza-
tion of the world in which all elements are made to
belong to a single super-family. Any food-procuring
act – whether hunting, fishing, or gathering – therefore implies an element of cannibalism. Such considerations placed people under a debt of obligation,
which had eventually to be repaid. At death, the body
returned to Earth Mother, who took it back to nourish
the plants that would in turn feed both people and
animals; the spirit, or soul, was released to be reborn.

CHAPTER THREE

Buffalo Hunters
of the Plains

•••••••••••

Comanche camp, buffalo hide tepee, *c*1870. Tepees were year-round dwellings for the nomadic Plains tribes, and were used by the semi-nomadic groups during buffalo hunts. The tepee was easy to transport. It was cool in summer and warm in winter, and could be kept smoke-free by altering the position of the flaps at the top.

Knife and sheath, Teton Sioux, before 1840. In porcupine quill work of this kind, the quills were first flattened and softened by biting, and were then dyed using a variety of natural minerals and plant juices. They were then pressed through holes made in a piece of hide.

THERE WAS ONE WORD that summed up the nature of the Plains and Prairies that lie at the heart of North America: buffalo. The immense grasslands, in which early pioneers measured distances in months rather than miles, extended from Texas up into Canada, and from the Rocky Mountain foothills across to the line of the Mississippi. They were, first and foremost, buffalo country. It was through the presence of this magnificent animal that the cultures of the Plains and Prairies Indians were created, and the senseless slaughter of the herds by White hunters was the ultimate reason these cultures declined.

It is difficult to look back and believe the rapidity with which the herds were destroyed; commercial hunting began only in 1872, and by 1885 the herds were gone. Even more difficult to comprehend is the staggering number of buffalo killed in these thirteen short years. Individual herds could contain as many as half a million animals, and early nineteenth-century documents mention the passage of travelers being blocked for days while herds passed. At times, paddle steamers were unable to navigate the Missouri River because of the numbers of buffalo swimming across, and the comment that the land was black with buffalo for as far as the eye could see is frequently encountered in the early travelers' reports.

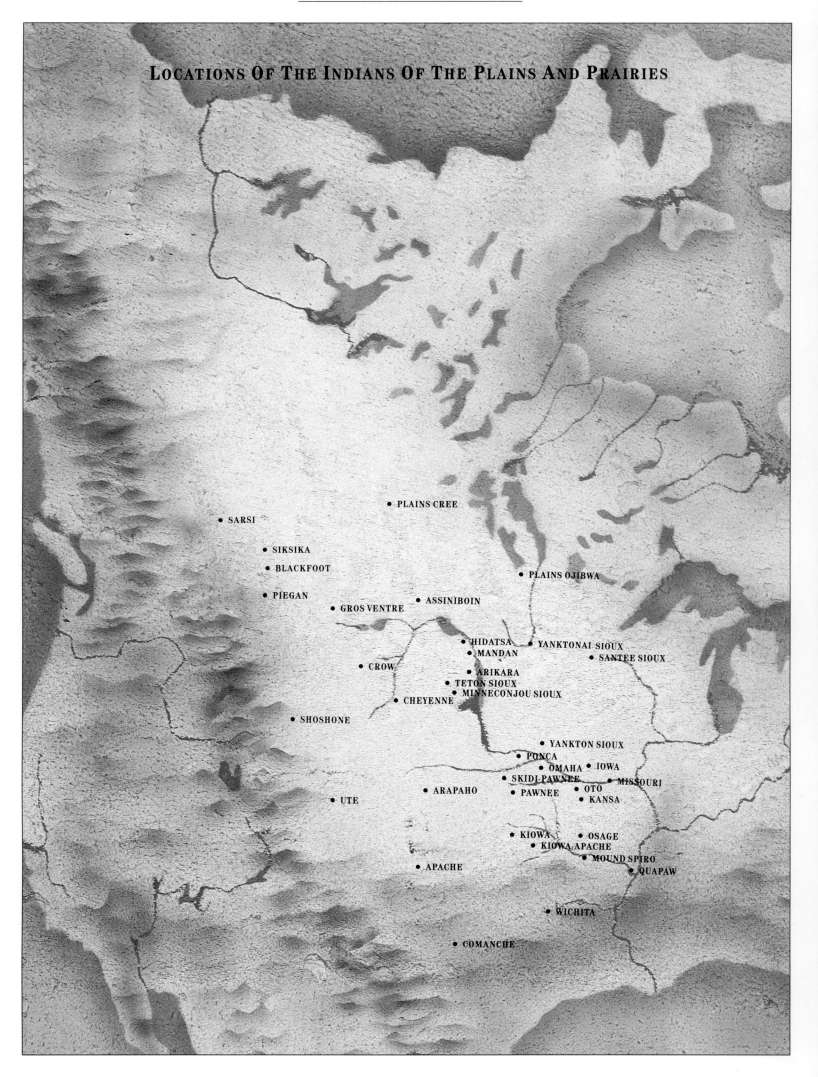

LOCATIONS OF THE INDIANS OF THE PLAINS AND PRAIRIES

PLAINS CREE

SARSI

SIKSIKA

BLACKFOOT

PLAINS OJIBWA

PIEGAN

GROS VENTRE   ASSINIBOIN

HIDATSA   YANKTONAI SIOUX
MANDAN   SANTEE SIOUX
CROW   ARIKARA
TETON SIOUX
MINNECONJOU SIOUX
CHEYENNE

SHOSHONE

YANKTON SIOUX
PONCA
OMAHA   IOWA
SKIDI-PAWNEE   MISSOURI
ARAPAHO   PAWNEE   OTO
UTE   KANSA

KIOWA   OSAGE
KIOWA-APACHE
MOUND SPIRO
APACHE   QUAPAW

WICHITA

COMANCHE

44

THE BUFFALO

To White hunters, the buffalo represented a quick profit from hides that produced quality leather and from bones that made fertilizer. To the Indians, the buffalo provided food, clothing, and shelter. Buffalo meat was the Indians' staple diet, eaten fresh in spring and summer, and dried in winter. Dressed buffalo skins made durable covers for tepees and clothing for winter wear. Buffalo robes could be worn and used as bedding. Rawhide was useful in the manufacture of shields and semirigid containers, and softer dressed hide provided the material for bags and pouches. Hair and sinew could be used in making ropes, bowstrings, and cording; horns and hoofs made ladles, spoons, and bowls, or could be boiled down as glue. The paunch was a useful watertight carrier, and the tail a handy fly whisk. Strong buffalo bones provided a variety of hide-scraping and fleshing tools. Even the dried dung, or buffalo chips, was the principal source of fuel for fires.

Buffalo were sacred and central to the ceremonial and social organization of the tribes. Because buffalo are migratory animals, they also dictated that all tribes had a nomadic lifestyle for at least part of the year. There were, however, two distinct cultural expressions of buffalo-dependent culture: that of the fully nomadic peoples of the western short-grass Plains, and that of the seminomadic village peoples of the eastern tall-grass Prairies.

PLAINS AND PRAIRIES

The nomadic, tepee-dwelling tribes of the northern part of the Plains are well known through popular literature, and include the Blackfoot, Crow, and Sioux. Further south were tribes who shared a very similar pattern of living such as the Cheyenne, Arapaho, Kiowa, and Comanche. To the east, in the Prairies, were several groups whose lifestyle was more sedentary than that of the true nomads. These people had permanent villages and planted crops of corn, beans, squash, and pumpkins. They wove reed mats, which they used for partitions and bedding instead of the skins used by the nomads. But they, too, spent a considerable part of the year in pursuit of the herds. The most northerly of the groups, the Hidatsa, Mandan, and Arikara, lived on the Missouri River. Further south, in what are now Nebraska and Kansas, and closer to the Mississippi, were several other village tribes, including the Omaha, Kansa, Ponca, Osage, and Quapaw. These spoke various Siouan dialects, and their traditions state they were at one time a single people. Also in the southern part of the region lived the Oto, Iowa, and Missouri, and the Caddoan-speaking Pawnee, Skidi, and Wichita.

New Fire, Kiowa, 1834. New Fire, described as a Kiowa band chief, was painted by George Catlin while on a visit to a Comanche village. He wears a boar's tusk amulet and a war whistle around his neck.

Kiowa beaded moccasins, early twentieth century. Beads were a sought after trade item from the first contacts with European traders, and were eventually to almost totally supplant the earlier use of dyed porcupine quills. Patterns were based initially on old quill designs.

The early histories of these various tribes are very different, and although the buffalo had been economically important in the region for at least 12,000 years, from when Ice-Age hunters pursued it, few of the tribes trace their origins to the grasslands. People came and went constantly, in great swirling migrations and movements that followed those of the herds, and most tribes moved into the area from elsewhere. The Blackfoot came from the Great Lakes, the Sioux

Moccasins, plains Cree, 1820. These very beautiful Moccasins, Plains Cree, one of the earliest examples of Northern Plains art in any collection. The high ankle flaps are a woodlands characteristic, reflecting styles originating in the forest homeland of the Cree tribes who moved onto the northern fringes of the Plains.

46

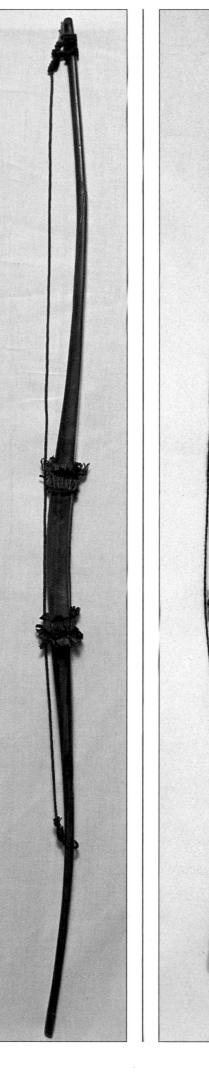

Recurved buffalo hunting bow, Crow, before 1850. This bow would have been used only during buffalo hunts and in parades. At other times, an inferior everyday bow would be used. At some time since this example was collected, the twisted sinew bowstring has been removed and refastened to the leading edge of the bow instead of to the rear.

Painted buffalo robe, Pawnee. Buffalo robes were of importance to the nomadic and semi-nomadic tribes of the Plains and Prairies, who used them for tepee covers, clothing, bedding, and as a means of recording their family history and their war exploits. This one explains the various achievements of its owner in pictographic form.

from the Eastern Woodlands, the Sarsi from the Subarctic. The Crow separated from the Hidatsa, who like the Mandan have links to earlier Plains Woodland cultures. The Pawnee, together with some of the Siouan-speaking peoples such as the Osage, have ties with the Caddo-Mississippians who built temple mounds at Mound Spiro in Oklahoma and who were themselves an immigrant group.

Some of these people first inhabited the grasslands a long time ago, but not in ancient times. Some tribes, such as the Cheyenne, who moved to the region within the historic period, arrived very recently. Perhaps only the Kiowa can claim antiquity. Prior to the adoption of the horse and gun in the second half of the eighteenth century, all the nomadic tribes lived as family bands of pedestrian hunters, severely limited in their material culture by the size of load their dogs could carry. Other groups occupied numerous small village settlements on the rivers of the east, where they planted crops and moved on foot into the grasslands for buffalo hunting.

THE HORSE AND THE GUN

The spread of horses from Sante Fe in the Southwest and of guns from the Northeast met on the Plains, and transformed the pedestrian hunters and farmers into mounted warriors almost overnight. Plains culture flared suddenly. Like a prairie fire, it had an awesome vitality, spontaneity, and energy, but was destined to burn itself out quickly. By 1890 the passionate and explosive response was over: the buffalo were virtually extinct, and the tribes had all been confined to reservations. For the seminomadic tribes, closer to White population centers, this had happened thirty years earlier. But with the nomads, the last of the tribes to come up against European and American expansion, this time marked the end of native American armed resistance.

In the 100 years or so that mounted nomadism flourished, however, it fired the imaginations of many people sufficiently to become the stereotype of the American Indian. When one thinks of Indians, the immediate image is of the Sioux warrior with his trailing feather war bonnet, painted pony, and fierce, warlike independence. It is an enduring image, made possible only because the horse enabled the potential of nomadism to be fully realized – travel was swifter and easier than anything the pedestrian hunters had experienced. At the same time, the gun permitted the formation of warrior élites, not because it replaced the traditional lance and bow – which continued to be used – but because it made the tribes more powerful and pushed them into headlong conflicts.

In all of this, the horse and gun were merely facilitators. The driving force behind the expansion of the

tribes was the grasslands itself, with its apparently endless space. Parra-wa-Samen, or Ten Bears, of the Yamparika Comanche, eloquently expressed this when he said, "I was born upon the prairies, where the wind blew free and there was nothing to break the light of the sun." It is easy to understand the forces that compelled him to speak this way. Even today it is possible in some areas to imagine that one's line of vision extends forever, and to gaze across rolling hills over which the constant wind sends continual ripples of motion through the grasses. These are lands that invite one to travel.

SEMI-NOMADS

Extensive contact with Europeans began with the semi-nomadic groups. These were powerful tribes, often consisting of several villages who considered

▲ ▬▬▬▬
Earth lodges, Pawnee, 1868–69. This Pawnee village on the Loup Form of the Platte River was photographed in the winter. The lodges were built from a timber framework which was covered with a layer of brush and sod, heaped over with earth, to create a permanent dwelling.

▼ ▬▬▬▬
Reed mat, Pawnee, 1920s. This mat is one of the only two surviving examples from the Pawnee, both of which were made in Oklahoma. Such mats were common in the earth lodges of the semi-nomadic tribes.

themselves allied. Although each village was essentially an autonomous unit, tribal ceremonies were held involving participants from the various settlements. Some tribes, like the Pawnee and Osage, lived in multifamily earth lodges constructed with a wooden framework over which sod was placed. The Wichita, who lived in river floodlands which encouraged the growth of particularly tall grasses, had reed-covered lodges. In areas closer to the Woodlands, lodges covered with bark were used.

Corn growing was as important to these semi-nomadic people as was buffalo hunting, and many of their rituals and ceremonies give corn and buffalo positions of equal importance. Migrations of buffalo determined their summer movements on to the Plains – when they traveled as complete tribes and lived in tepees – but corn dictated when the summer hunts began and ended. The people could not leave their

Inlaid pipe bowl, Pawnee, early nineteenth century. This Pawnee pipe is carved from catlinite, a soft red stone found only in Minnesota and traded widely among the Plains tribes for pipe-making.

Buffalo Bull, The Cheyenne, Bird-That-Goes-To-War, Pawnee, 1832. These three warriors were among the Pawnees whom George Caitlin painted at Fort Leavenworth in 1832. They all have shaved heads and wear red roach head-dresses. By their distinctive facepaints, these warriors can be recognized as Pawnee, but the symbols themselves, such as the hand, have a wider significance. The hand is representative of a powerful life force and could only be used by a prominent warrior.

villages until the crop had been planted, and they had to be back in time for the harvest. The stability of the village also enabled certain individuals to gain status through a form of hereditary rank, and it was often an advantage to a young man to have parents in high positions. Yet leadership was essentially democratic and supported by popular opinion.

In addition to being a member of the tribe, each individual was often also a member of a moiety, a sub-division of the tribe into two more or less equal parts. Each moiety had responsibilities for different aspects of tribal life. They formed a complementary pair, each half of which had the same objective in mind, the unity of the tribe and its security. But they pursued these aims from opposite poles; by bringing these opposites together, a balance, or harmony, could be achieved that did not give undue emphasis to the aims of either. Beyond this, each person was a member of a clan that felt itself bound together through blood relationships.

All these divisions had prominent members whose views and opinions would be listened to with respect, and who often acted as spokesmen for the group. White people erroneously thought of such people as "chiefs," while at the same time frequently confusing clans, moieties, and tribes. This led to an impression of a bewildering array of chiefs with "authority" extending over any number of disparate groups of people who considered themselves related in several ways.

Each tribe also had a number of societies, consisting of people who felt a common bond. Some were age-graded, in that all members belonged to the same age range; others depended on achievement, as in the Warrior Societies where admission was through the performance of particuarly daring acts of courage; still others were ceremonial, related to the performance of particular rituals such as growing sacred tobacco. Each of these had its leading members or spokesmen, who again could be conceived as "chiefs."

Parallel to these were the shamanic societies or fraternities, whose members each combined the roles of philospher, magician, tribal historian, doctor, and

Little White Bear, Kansa, 1832. Big Elk, Omaha, 1832. Little White Bear and Big Elk were painted by George Catlin while visiting Forth Leavenworth. They were part of the ancient tradition that linked many of the semi-nomadic tribes to earlier cultural expressions of the Southeast, for instance, the practice of shaving the head and wearing a roach.

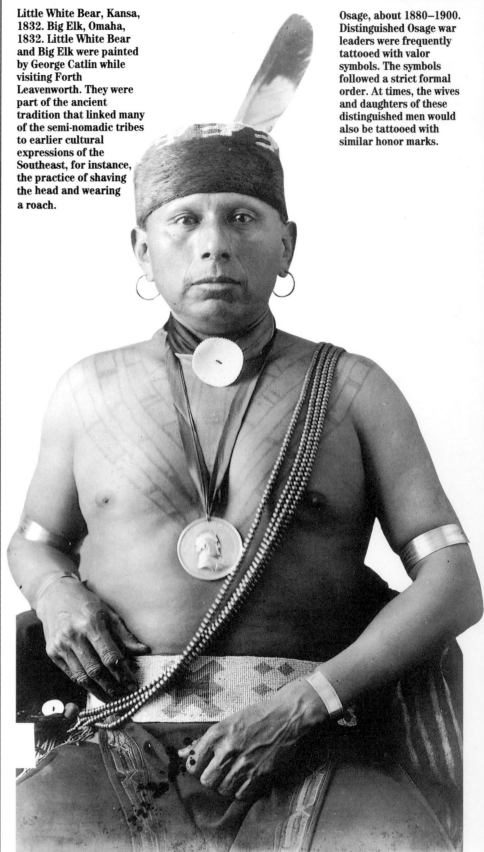

Osage, about 1880–1900. Distinguished Osage war leaders were frequently tattooed with valor symbols. The symbols followed a strict formal order. At times, the wives and daughters of these distinguished men would also be tattooed with similar honor marks.

Engraved shell gorget, Caddo-Mississippian, Mound Spiro, c1200–1400. The expansion of Southern Death Cult Mississippians onto the Plains reached as far as Mound Spiro in Oklahoma. The Cult spider emblem on this engraved shell is, however, similar to the spider tattooed on the backs of Osage women's hands.

▲ ▬▬▬▬▬▬
Painted Robe, Sioux,
*c*1830. This so-called
"Box and Border Design"
was widely worn by Sioux
women. The red and black
painted elements
symbolize the important
stages of a woman's life,
and are also linked with
the buffalo.

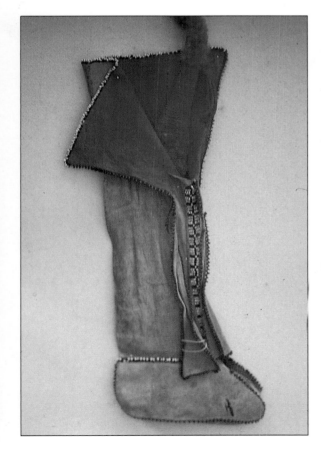

◄ ▬▬▬▬▬▬
Paint bag, Osage.
Pigments used for
personal adornment and
for painting on hides and
skins were kept in dry,
powdered form in special
paint bags. In use, a little
of the crushed pigment
was mixed with grease or
fat to bind it and to cause
it to adhere to the surface
on which it was applied.

priest. It was through the shamans that the various divisions exercised their sacred duty to perform rituals that guaranteed the continuance of the tribe and promoted its well-being. Rituals often also referred back to the origin of a tribe. Among the Skidi, for instance, a number of "medicine bundles" – skin or cloth wrappings containing tokens of spiritual power – were held in separate villages and referred to the belief that the structure and order of the tribe were organized by the stars. The powers above made them into villages and families, and taught them how to live and how to perform their ceremonies. Village life was minutely detailed and well-ordered, with certain prescribed or proscribed courses of action in any particular situation, but nevertheless contained a series of options for every individual.

NOMADS

Similar ideas were held by the nomadic tribes of the western part of the region, who also had fraternities of shamans, clans, moieties, and Warrior Societies. But here the need to be constantly moving shifted the social focus from the village to the band. Much of the year was spent in small, mobile bands with democratic leadership. Decisions affecting the band were made in councils at which any member could express an opinion. Nobody was bound by anything with which he disagreed, and even the most prominent members of the community had no authority over anyone else. The result was a series of flexible units with changing populations, and with close marriage and blood ties to several other groups in the vicinity.

Each group was autonomous and independent, but considered itself related to other bands both through family ties and by similarities in custom and language. An aggregation of these groups is generally referred to as a tribe, although this does not imply any political cohesiveness. In early summer, several separate bands would start moving together for the major buffalo hunts and so that the annual tribal renewal ceremonies could take place. At such times, they formed circle-camps, so named because tepees were pitched in a circle, leaving a central area free in which ceremonies could take place. The circle was also a sacred statement of the people's belief. A circle permits continual movement, as it has neither beginning nor end, but it is also an enclosing form that protects and that expresses the wholeness of a group. Several hundred families might gather at one of these camps, in much the same way as the separate villages of the semi-nomads came together for tribal purposes.

MEN AND WOMEN

For most of the time, the world of both the Plains and Prairies tribes was, to all intents and purposes, that of the individual; one in which honor and respect were gained through personal merit and skill. A man strove to be a great warrior and hunter, a hero among a nation of heroes. It was, superficially at least, a man's world. But this overlooks the fact that women owned everything to do with the household and the domestic sphere of life; that a man's total possessions were the clothes he wore and the weapons he carried.

Rather than being communities in which women were subordinated, as they are so often depicted, these were communities in which the roles of the sexes were precisely defined. Clear statements were made about the interdependence of men and women, and about the ways in which either could gain distinction and wear marks of merit. Painting and tattooing were signal devices of respect and status. Among

▲ ▬▬▬▬▬
Grass lodge, Wichita, before 1900. The Wichita, living on the banks of the Arkansas River, had access to extensive stands of reeds and grasses which they used in making thatched coverings for their lodges and shelters. The beehive shaped house shown here was used as living accommodation.

▲ ▬▬▬▬▬
Wild Sage, Wichita girl, 1834. Painted by George Catlin, Wild Sage is wearing a skin cloak. It was common for Wichita women to wear only a skirt or apron before European conceptions of modesty introduced the full-length dress.

▶ ▬▬▬▬▬
Sewing awl, Iowa. Quill- and beadwork on hide was accomplished by first piercing the hide with an awl to create a hole through which the quills could be pushed or the sinew strands holding the beads could be threaded. The awl shown here has a carved bone handle and a metal point that has been fashioned from an old file. Awls had many other uses.

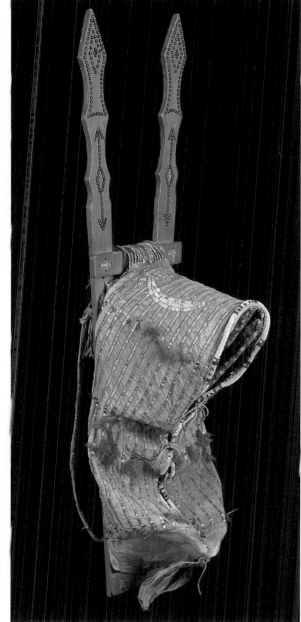

Kiowa girls, nineteenth century. These two Kiowa girls wear decorated buckskin dresses covered with a profusion of beads and cut fringes. They hold a fully beaded cradleboard that is also decorated with brass studs and inset mirrors.

Quanah Parker, Comanche, before 1870. The Kwahadi Comanche war leader, Quanah Parker, fought a desperate battle to prevent the southern herds of buffalo from being wiped out. He was the last of the Comanche chiefs to surrender. He is shown here wearing an eagle feather war bonnet.

Cradleborad, Kiowa. Babies were protected by being placed in cradleboards made from a wood frame with soft buckskin covers, and padded with moss. The cradleboard shown here has rich quillwork decoration, which includes a stylized buffalo on the projecting upper portion which served as a sunshade.

the Omaha, for instance, the symbol of the sun, with its promise of life-giving power, was a girl's tattooed mark of honor, corresponding with the tattooed markings used by the men to depict their skills in war and their ability to protect the people.

Away from the public displays, when emotions were deliberately concealed, Plains families were close and compassionate, with many expressions of affection and humor. Even so, warfare was a constant preoccupation, and every young man eagerly sought war honors so that he might rise in status in the estimation of his peers and of the tribe. To understand this, we need to put the European conception of warfare aside. There was no desire to defeat an enemy or gain territory. Plains warfare derived from an environment where individual skills meant the difference between survival and death. Such skills were the ability to act decisively, to show oneself capable of responding immediately to whatever circumstance presented itself, and to be able to deal with anything that threatened the security of the band.

WARRIORS

The Plains warrior set out to prove he could overcome danger and that he was able to protect the people from forces that derived either from the environment or from man. The more bravery he

demonstrated, the greater the protection he could offer. A leading warrior gained respect and status within the tribe, and his achievements were recognized through elaborate coded systems of honors: the way an eagle feather was worn, paint markings on his horse, details of costume, and the right to aspire to a high position in an élite Warrior Society.

Bravery rather than aggression was recognized, and killing rarely featured prominently in the order of war honors. It was far more dangerous to dash across open country against an armed opponent and to merely touch him than to make an attempt at killing or disarming; among all the tribes, such an act ranked more highly than any other. Scalping expeditions were organized only after extensive preparations under the guidance of a shaman and were matters of serious concern. They atoned for the loss of a member of one's own tribe when, by bringing back a scalp, a period of mourning could be ritually closed and grief transferred elsewhere. The scalp was, therefore, an honorific emblem and not a war trophy, and among many tribes it was spoken of as a "friend."

By far the majority of war parties were horse-raiding expeditions conducted by small groups of warriors intent on proving their daring. These expeditions were of importance primarily to the individuals who engaged in them. Ownership of horses made it possible to give valuable exchange presents at marriage,

Parfleche, Sioux, 1820. Parfleche cases of painted rawhide were used for the storage and transportation of pemmican, the dried strips of buffalo meat that were kept as a winter store. The pemmican was placed in the centre of the parfleche, which was then folded around it and laced with rawhide thongs.

Buffalo hide shield, before 1850. This shield is made from the thick neck skin of a buffalo bull, and is strong enough to deflect a bullet from a muzzle-loading rifle. It owes its protective power, however, to the painted design with a buffalo inspired by a vision of its owner.

Dog Society dancer, Minnetaree, 1833–34. Pehrioska-Ruhpa, one of the four principals of the Minnetaree Dog Society – a group who shared a common vision in which the dog endowed them with his power – posed for this portrait by Karl Bodmer in full Society regalia.

honoring both the girl and her family. Horses might also be lent to the poor and elderly when camp was moved, showing one's own generosity. Generosity, selflessness, and a concern for the welfare of the less fortunate were accorded the same importance as courage. The bravest of warriors, if he acted recklessly and only from self-interest, would never gain the admiration of the tribe and would be unable to obtain an honored position in the tribal councils.

THE BUFFALO HUNT

Warfare was a means of enhancing individual standing within the tribe and conceived as a challenge to oneself; yet it was governed and controlled by the overriding concerns of the community as a whole. Similar conceptions applied to the annual buffalo hunts, which were often equated with war. Recognition of individual skills was achieved through arrows marked with personal insignia, but the hunt itself was under the control of a Warrior Society who determined when the hunters would leave the camps and what strategies they would use.

In the early days, before the herds had been decimated, hunts were generally successful – although, should the herds prove evasive, rituals for calling the buffalo might be held under the auspices of a prominent shaman. Several hunting methods were employed. The chase, in which a stampeded herd was pursued by hunters mounted on buffalo-runners (highly trained horses renowned for their fleetness of foot, courage, and ability to respond instantly to a rider's commands) were the most thrilling and most popular. Surrounds might be used where there was a possibility of the herd becoming too scattered; hunters would encircle the herd, which milled helplessly, unable to break through the circle. Especially in the approach

Signal pipes, Assiniboine and Mandan, 1820–30. Bone signal pipes were used by members of war parties to maintain contact, and were also blown in an attack. Similar pipes are reported for tribes such as the Sioux, who wore them tied above the ear so that as a warrior galloped towards his opponent the inrush of air caused the pipe to sound.

Tobacco pouch, Eastern Sioux, collected 1820. This richly decorated tobacco pouch is in the style of the Woodlands/ Great Lakes, an area from which Sioux tribes were forced by pressure from the Chippewa.

to winter when the herds had thinned, a *piskun*, or buffalo-jump, might be employed. This involved a controlled stampede toward a natural obstacle such as a high ledge. The herd would be unable to avoid the danger and provided piles of hides from which tepee covers and winter robes for clothing and bedding could be made.

SUN DANCES

Much of the meat obtained on the annual hunts was dried for use as a winter supply, but there was plenty of fresh meat to support feasts and social gatherings. Prized buffalo tongues were consecrated for use in sacred rituals, especially those of the major annual renewal ceremonies in which the world was "made over." For convenience, such rituals of the nomadic tribes are referred to as "sun dances," from the Sioux reference to "gazing at the sun" during their celebrations. In fact, most of these rituals did not involve any sun worship.

For the Cheyenne, the prominent feature of renewal ceremonies was the sacred earths. Spiral patterns were drawn in cleared patches to absorb spirit influences; the spirals would later be reversed so that spirit power might be disseminated to the people. Among the Crow, the central object of veneration was a sacred doll, representing the mythical child that brought spirit blessings. The Sioux invested this power in the sacred buffalo, relating it to warriors who endured self-torture. The Blackfoot conception passed these powers to the Sacred Woman. It was she who married Morning Star, from whom she obtained the sacred Natoas containing all the elements needed to provide the tribe's continued success. It was only when her son, Scarface, defeated the monster birds threatening Sun's existence, however, that her power could be fully realized.

Among the seminomadic groups, the conceptions were different. They related to both buffalo and corn, but still referred back to an overall unifying force. The Osage had a series of seven war ceremonies, which were linked with those of peace to create a harmonious whole. Among the Mandan, the Okipa combined the individualistic aspects of warrior power with that of the all-important buffalo. Their ceremonies demanded sacrifice from pledged individuals to show their endurance, but relied on the life-sustaining qualities of the buffalo to guarantee the continued well-being and fertility of the tribe.

With the Skidi, power was drawn from separate tribal medicine bundles holding tokens of the spirit forces. These could be ritually reanimated. The powers they contained could be combined and unified within the separate villages by a specific Bundle Priest, or brought together under the auspices of the

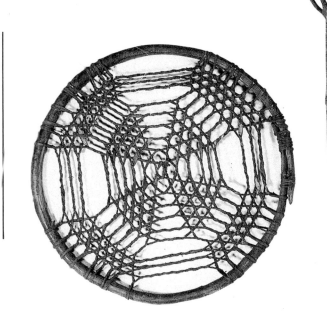

Gaming hoop, Mandan, 1830. This gaming hoop has a wooden rim which is laced with sinew netting. It was used as part of a popular game that the Mandan shared with many other tribes of the region. The hoop, representing the female principle, was rolled between two warriors who attempted to catch it on long poles, representing the male principle.

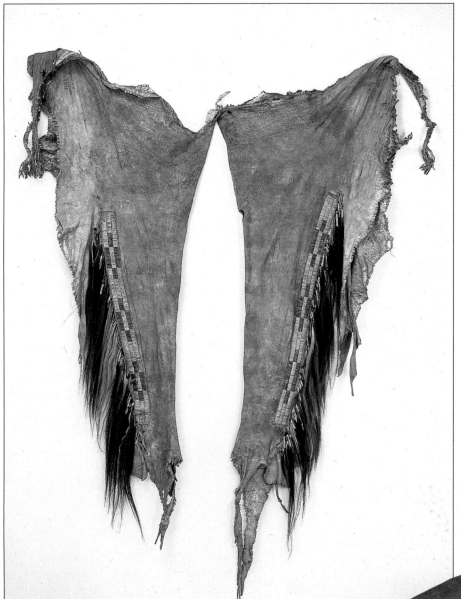

demanded, and only the strongest would receive the vision he sought. If he were fortunate, a dream animal would appear to teach him the songs and ritual.

WINTER TALES

In late summer, the circle-camps of the nomads broke up, and the bands moved back to traditional camping grounds along the sheltered river banks. At the same time, the semi-nomads returned to the security of their villages for the fall harvest. Winter would be spent gathered closely around the fires in the tepees and lodges, listening to the tales and myths that it was considered unlucky to tell during the summer months, when energy had to be expended on more immediate economic needs.

It was through the tales that the people were reminded of why the world had been created, and their responsibilities and duties were defined. But the tales had different meanings according to whom they were being told. For the children, they taught the ways of the people and animals, and explained the need to show respect and never to take more than was needed. Young warriors learned about their role as protectors and of the importance of constant vigilance. Girls were reminded that chastity and purity were sacred and that, ultimately, they carried the life of the tribe. The middle-aged listened carefully, trying to under-

Evening Star Priest, who alone had knowledge of all the different bundle ceremonies. His role was a passive one – he never conducted ceremonies – but his understanding was the most powerful because he brought together the elements of Earth and Sky. Skidi ceremonialism, based on an intricate cosmology, is said to be the most complex in North America.

PERSONAL VISIONS

Individually, every man, and occasionally some women, attempted to contact the spirit powers and acquire some form of supernatural spirit protection. Acquisition of power was through the vision quest. The seeker would go to the top of a high bluff that was the home of the ancestors. Here, surrounded by relics of the past, he attempted to contact the spirits through fasting and by offering smoke from a sacred pipe, requesting a token from them, and asking for knowledge of songs and facepaint that could be used to reanimate their gift in the future. The spirits did not give this easily; they had to be challenged and power

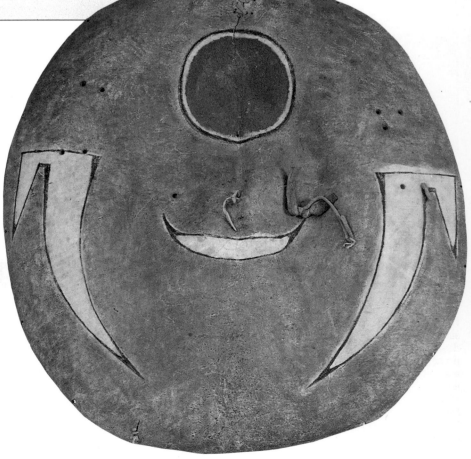

Leggings, Yanktonai Sioux, 1820. These leggings are made from pronghorn antelope skin and have quilled strips from which hair-locks are suspended. The hair denotes the wearer as a prominent warrior, and much of it would have derived from enemy scalps. These would have been divided separate locks for attachment to the leggings.

Shield, Palins Cree. This buffalo hide shield bears visionary images of a very abstract nature, but which seem to relate to the celestial powers. The central figures may well be depictions of the Sun and Moon, which can be interpreted as ensuring a long life. It is unusual, however, for the sun to be used in this way.

stand the deeper meanings that the stories contained, meanings that offered glimpses of the mysteries and of the world of the spirits.

The Elders, who told the tales, reminisced and looked back to previous winters. Their thoughts were with the powers that traveled through the land, of the buffalo, the pronghorn antelope, the grizzly bear, and the myriad other creatures with which they shared the land. But, mostly, they considered the events of the previous year and considered carefully whether the people had followed the "true path" that had been laid down for them by the ancients.

Buffalo Bull's Back Fat, Blackfoot, 1832. This magnificently dressed man was Head Chief of the Blood division of the Blackfoot when George Catlin painted him. His deerskin clothing is decorated with porcupine quillwork, as is the stem of the pipe he is holding.

CHAPTER FOUR

Fishermen of the Northwest Coast

THE NORTHWEST COAST is a region of mystery and magic. Dense mists and high rainfall disguise the shapes of the giant cedars, turning them into vague forms with a ghostly presence. It is an area of rocky inlets and fjords in which water, land, and sky blend as one continuous form; where the distinction between solids and liquids can never be fully comprehended. High humidity rots fallen trees and then carpets them densely with moss to create the illusion of solid ground, but it is ground that is treacherous and bears no weight. This narrow, rugged strip of temperate rainforest, often little more than 50 miles (80 kilometers) wide, extends for 1,200 miles (1,900 kilometers) along the shores of British Columbia and southern Alaska. It is permanently isolated from the rest of the continent by the great peaks of the Coast and Rocky Mountains.

A LAND OF SPIRITS

It was an appropriate abode for Tsonoqua, the Wild Woman of the Woods, whose call could be heard whenever the wind sighed through the topmost

Painted house front, Kwakiutl, before 1899. This plank house was photographed at Nimkish village on Alert Bay, Vancouver Island. Vertical planking suggests the house was already old when the photograph was taken, because horizontal boarding had been in vogue for some time prior to 1900. The painting depicts the Thunderbird carrying off a whale.

branches of the trees. She would entice children away from their homes. Her husband, Bokwus, gathered the souls of those who had drowned in the dangerous whirlpools and eddies that run between the countless islands. Komokwa, the Lord of the Oceans, resided in a house supported by the seals and could command the killer whales to hunt for him. Here lived also Hoxhok, the Monster Bird, and Baxbakualanuxsiwae, the Cannibal-at-the-North-End-of-the-World. They inspired the Hamatsa Society dancers and caused them to act recklessly and behave as ghosts. Even Echo was the voice of the dead, repeating careless words spoken too loudly by the living.

These coastal reaches were home to a number of tribes speaking unrelated languages, but who formed an exceptionally homogenous group. The natural barriers of their land prevented major influences from other areas. In the south were the Coast Salish tribes of Vancouver Island and the adjacent mainland. Sharing Vancouver Island with them were some Kwakiutl groups and, on the seaward shores, the Nootka. Other Kwakiutl speakers lived on the mainland, and north of them, opposite the Queen Charlotte Islands were

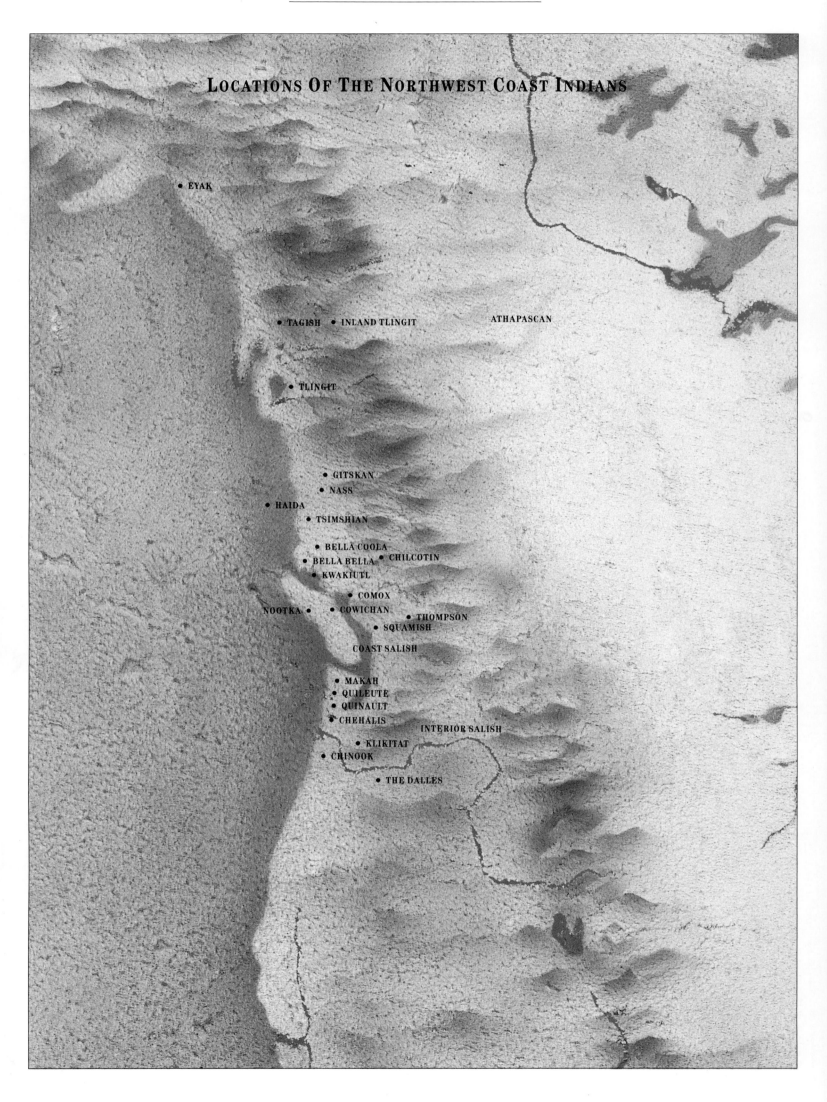

LOCATIONS OF THE NORTHWEST COAST INDIANS

• EYAK

• TAGISH   • INLAND TLINGIT   ATHAPASCAN

• TLINGIT

• GITSKAN
• NASS
• HAIDA
• TSIMSHIAN

• BELLA COOLA
• BELLA BELLA   • CHILCOTIN
• KWAKIUTL

• COMOX
NOOTKA •   • COWICHAN
            • THOMPSON
         • SQUAMISH

COAST SALISH

• MAKAH
• QUILEUTE
• QUINAULT
• CHEHALIS   INTERIOR SALISH
   • KLIKITAT
• CHINOOK

• THE DALLES

LOCATIONS OF THE NORTHWEST COAST INDIANS

Mask, Tsimshian or
Tlingit, nineteenth
century. The mask is that
of a shaman's animal-
familiar, combining
human and animal
attributes. The mask is
finished with a lead polish
to reflect light from the
fire during performances.

the Bella Coola. The Queen Charlotte Islands themselves were occupied by the Haida. The other main tribes had villages on the river inlets and islands farther north; they were the Tsimshian and Tlingit.

All these people were profoundly influenced by spirit powers associated with distant human-animal ancestors of their clans. These spirit powers gave supernatural protection in the form of totem privileges. Such powerful ancestors as Eagle, Raven, Killer Whale, or Wolf created a stable background in Northwest Coast culture. Early European explorers

Totem pole, possibly Bella Coola, nineteenth century. This totem pole, although it has lost much of its paint, still presents an imposing spectacle. The figure depicted here is probably Beaver, but because the prominent incisor teeth that normally characterize Beaver are missing, it could also be a bear that has caught a fish.

and traders were astonished and impressed when they first came to this region and saw the masssive plank houses. The houses lined the top of steep beaches along the river inlets, their fronts painted with images of the clan totems. Rows of carved and painted welcoming figures, palms outstretched to show they carried no weapons, stood in front of the houses. The forms of the figures were sharply delineated against the dense greens of the forests that climbed abruptly away behind the villages and disappeared into the mists.

TOTEM FIGURES

Everything these people possessed was embellished with totem figures. House posts were elaborately carved and later developed into towering totem poles when the Indians acquired metal-bladed tools. Also carved were dugout canoes, wooden storage boxes, sleeping platforms, bowls and dishes, ladles, spoons, even fishhooks. On materials that did not lend themselves to carving, such as the shredded cedar bark mats and capes, blankets woven from mountain sheep wool and dog hair, and basketwork, the totems were applied by using colored reeds and grasses, dyed wool, or paint.

Although no surface was left blank and no space remained unfilled by these highly stylized representations, this was never a purely decorative art. A bird figure carved into a translucent ladle made from steamed and bent mountain sheep horn, for example, transformed the object into something that contained magical properties of its own. In this instance, the simple act of serving food restated the link with the ancestral forces and with the other members of one's clan. Even a stranger from a different tribe and speaking a different language would find shelter and protection among people sharing his own clan affiliation. Paintings and carvings told him or her immediately which houses would offer a friendly reception and those where he or she would be unwelcome.

SUMMER VILLAGES

The village sites just described were occupied only during Tsetseka, the sacred winter season. In spring, the people moved to summer villages close to salmon-bearing rivers and near the berrying grounds. Salmon spawn in these rivers in such prodigious numbers that summer fishing provided the staple diet of most of the tribes. Huge quantities of surplus fish could be dried and used at feasts in the winter when the major rituals took place. The waters provided other resources, such as halibut, eulachon, and shellfish, which were important in the diet, and the Nootka even practiced harpoon whaling from dugout canoes. Kelp was eaten, as were other seaweeds; roots, seeds, and berries could be gathered easily. Occasional inland game animals, such as deer and bear, supplemented what was almost exclusively a marine economy.

POTLATCHES

The resources of this country were so rich that winter could be devoted almost entirely to ceremonial and social activity. This gave rise to a leisured class in which status and rank were inherited and associated

House posts, Coast Salish, nineteenth century. These posts were part of a series that once supported the roof of the massive Cowichan meeting house near modern Duncan, Vancouver Island. They depict figures holding otters. The Otter, as one of the Original People, was ancestral to the Cowichan and held in sacred reverence.

with the right to own and display certain privileges. These rights, however, had to be validated, and the principal means of doing so was through gift-giving during potlatches. Small potlatches were held for the validation of lesser rights, to celebrate a girl's ear-piercing or to mark the acquisition of an adult name at puberty. For lower ranking people, this merely required inviting close family and giving gifts in recognition of their attendance.

Status generally determined the number of guests at a potlatch, as well as the involvement of the other clan and family members. For the validation of the highest ranking positions – for example, when the son of a clan leader took over status from one of his parents – it might be felt necessary to invite related clans from other villages. The number of gifts distributed was a reflection of the importance of the position being validated, as well as of the generosity of the host family.

For large potlatches, the guests arrived from the sea in huge dugout canoes – some capable of carrying thirty or forty people – which were brilliantly painted and had great carved prows depicting the totem of the clan to which they belonged. A costumed figure, representing the Bear, Eagle, Thunderbird, or other prominent ancestor in the clan's mythology, danced at the prow to the rhythmic chanting of the crew and the hypnotic beating of their paddles on the gunwales of the boat. The simultaneous arrival of several such canoes was a powerful and impressive statement of a clan's strength and solidarity.

The guests would be met on the beach by the host clan and ceremoniously led to the clan house. Here, seated in order of status on raised tiers around the walls, they listened to lengthy speeches that told the clan's history. These were tales of how in ancient days an ancestor had been instructed by a spirit, such as Bear, Beaver, or Eagle. The spirit had passed on supernatural power and given the ancestor a privileged right to display this through the wearing of a particular mask and the performance of a certain dance. These rights of display were handed down through the generations, and the potlatch celebrated their transfer from a previous to a new owner.

Chief's daughter, Salish, early nineteenth century. The mat coverings on the walls of the house and the designs on the baskets suggest the family were living towards the interior, along the Columbia River, from where they would have traded regularly at the Dalles with their linguistic relatives on the coast.

Basket, Salish. The basket shown here is of a large type that was used for the storage of food products. Pattern is achieved by weaving in darker-colored natural materials rather than by using dyes.

DANCE SOCIETIES

Although the potlatch was essentially secular, it nevertheless featured prominently in rituals of a more sacred character. This was because the rituals, together with the associated dance masks, costumes, names, and songs, were all considered to be a form of property owned by a dance society. The membership of these societies paralleled that of the clan and had similar ranked positions. Admission to these positions had to be validated by the distribution of goods. Considerable amounts could be involved for the highest ranking positions, to which only the sons of leading clan members could aspire.

Society dances reached their greatest development among the Kwakiutl, Tsimshian, and Tlingit, and were pure drama and high theater. The most spectacular were the dances of the Hamatsa Society, whose members were inspired by the Cannibal Spirits. These dances took place within the leading clan house which had been ritually cleansed and prepared. They marked the adoption of a new initiate into the Society and were intended to shock.

Disembodied voices sounded from the depths of the fires, and spirit figures flew across the room at head height. Nan, the Grizzly Bear Dancer, barred the entrance to the house while Nunltsistalal, the

Hamatsa dancer, Kwakiutl, early nineteenth century. This member of the Hamatsa Society is wearing ceremonial regalia. His head-ring and neck-ring are woven from shredded Red cedar bark, symbolic of Society membership. Red cedar bark was sacred and could only be used during the winter tsetseka season.

Masked dance, Kwakiutl, early nineteenth century. This photograph shows many of the supernatural animal figures that inspired the Kwakiutl. Among the dancers in the foreground are the mythical Raven, with his long pointed beak, and the Thunderbird, with a shorter, curved beak.

Fire-Thrower, took live coals from the fire with his bare hands and recklessly threw them about. Meanwhile, the Chewing Spirit Dancer prowled through the village destroying valuable property and threatening anyone who came too close. A young woman, Kinqalalala, danced naked carrying a corpse to entice the Hamatsas; the initiate, excited at her appearance and unable to control the spirit by which he was possessed, would bite at the arms of spectators before being restrained and led to a room at the rear of the house to recover. The initiate would reappear several times to dance, growing visibly stronger until he was eventually able to control the spirit and could be admitted into the Society.

Everything in this performance used artifice. The voices came from the fires by way of kelp stems laid beneath the floor; the spirit figures were puppets; the corpse was an effigy. Even the damage and injury was arranged in advance and suitable compensation agreed – this would be paid at a later date at a potlatch that the Hamatsa Society sponsored.

Similar, but higher, payments were also made at the other major dance series of the Kwakiutl, the Dluwulaxa, or Those-Who-Descend-From-The-Heavens. The positions at the Dluwulaxa dances had even greater status and might require a series of potlatches. These dances did not have the furious energy inspired by the Cannibals, yet they were equally impressive. The dancers wore huge segmented masks, carved and painted, some so large that an assistant was required to support the weight. The masks represented the animal ancestors of the people. One dancer might mimic the undulating motions of the Killer Whale, while another darted fervently back and forth in the guise of Mosquito. The nature of many of the masks derived from the moss-laden country, where the true character of something could be hidden behind a different face. A dancer wearing a somber mask might, by pulling on concealed strings to open it, suddenly reveal an inner Sun.

In both the Hamatsa and Dluwulaxa Societies, the number of privileged positions was limited, so initiation could only occur on the retirement of an existing member. Because status was jealously guarded, dance positions were often handed down from a father to his son. This perpetuated a situation in which both social and ceremonial positions of rank were generally held by the same individuals. Demonstrations of privilege could only be acted out by men, but often, particularly among the northern tribes, the system of descent was matriarchal: men "danced out" power that was actually owned and inherited through the female lines of the tribe.

Nimkish village, Kwakiutl. Of special interest in this early engraving is the absence of totem poles, which developed after iron tools became available. Also of interest is the terraced nature of the village; clans owned particular house sites, and as populations expanded new houses were built above the original one.

Crooked-Beak mask, Kwakiutl, 1915. Masks such as this were part of the Hamatsa Society dance series, and represented supernatural creatures. Prominent among these was Galokwudzuwis, Crooked-Beak-of-Heaven, whose mask is shown here. Unlike most Hamatsa masks, that of Crooked-Beak is said to have been worn by women.

Raven mask, Kwakiutl, nineteenth century. Raven features prominently in the mythology and ritual of the Kwakiutl, and is often represented in masks. Some of these were articulated. That shown here has an opening beak and long hinged tongue. The eye, as shown in the detail photographs, can be made to open or close.

Button blanket, Tsimshian, c1900. After the introduction of European trade items, many ceremonial cloaks were made from trade cloth rather than mountain goat hair and dog hair. Mother-of-pearl buttons were often used in place of the earlier shell discs, giving these cloaks their popular name of "button blankets".

SPIRIT SINGING

The displays of the southern Coast Salish had a very different character from those of the central and northern areas. There were few masked dances, and only Swaie-Swaie, a creator figure in the form of a supernatural bird that descended into a lake, had a distinctive mask. The right to wear this mask was inherited through the leading families and needed to be validated. Other dances, however, derived from visions as a consequence of personal spirit contact, rather than from ancient privileges handed down from the ancestors. These "dramatizations of dreams" were highly individual and required no prior manifestations. As such, they were able to operate outside the framework of the rank-ordered dance positions found elsewhere.

Even though the visions were personal ones, the spirits contacted through them could be ordered into generic classes, such as the Animal, Water, or Mountain Spirits. Each of these classes had a distinctive drum rhythm with which it was associated. During performances, which are sometimes referred to as "spirit singing," the rhythms were used to induce trances through which the dancer and spirit were brought into a state of compatibility and harmony. This was something far removed from the inherent rivalry implied in the status performances elsewhere. The personal nature of the visions effectively prevented spirit singing from being substantially altered by the passage of history, and these dances persist to the present day in a virtually unchanged form.

THE WOLF DANCE

Among the Nootka, who were fiercely independent and conservative, was preserved what is perhaps the ancestral Society dance form for all those of the coast. This was the Nutlam, or Wolf Dance, which recorded the days when the wolves taught the people to live together in communities and gave them the hierarchies that were important in human societies. This dance featured the carrying away of a novice by the wolves. He would be taught their customs, rituals, and songs so that he might impart this knowledge to

▲ ▬▬▬▬▬▬
Portrait mask, Haida, *c*1825–1875. This mask has abstract paint on the face indicative of the clan facepaint that would have been worn by the person whom it represents. Such masks were worn during potlatches by individuals of high status and demonstrated the privileges handed down through the family.

▲ ▶ ▬▬▬▬▬
House posts, Haida, nineteenth century. Haida carvers were renowned for the subtlety and delicacy of their monumental carving, which was often painted with simple highlights in black and red as opposed to the multi-colored painting of the Kwakiutl and Bella Coola. The posts shown here have lost any paint they might once have had.

◀ ▬▬▬▬▬
Walrus-ivory carving, possibly Tlingit, nineteenth century. This carved object is pierced so that it can be suspended and is similar to pendants attached to necklaces worn by Tlingit shamans. If it is such an object, then it is likely to have been used as a head-scratching stick, although similar forms were also worn as nose pins.

70
●●●

the people on his return. It is significant that the land of the wolves was a distant one, buried in the depths of mythological time and referring to the human-animal ancestors. By utilizing this knowledge gained from the wolves in the present, the Nootka tied themselves firmly to the past.

During Nutlam, the wolves and the novice conversed in a language that was unintelligible to the uninitiated. Similar usage of "ancient" language to depict spirit contact is apparent in the curing rituals of Northwest Coast shamans, who inherited their skills as others inherited rank and privilege. The shamans' powers were not those of the clan totems, which were expressed in a secular context. These powers nevertheless derived from the same period of human-animal cohabitation. For a shaman to be effective, it was often necessary to make a spiritual journey back to a place where he and the spirits were able to converse.

SUPERNATURAL JOURNEYS

Most illnesses that could not be cured by herbal methods were conceived as resulting from "soul-loss." In such cases a shaman would attempt to recapture the lost soul before it traveled back to the land of the dead. If illness were slight, he might perceive the soul hovering near the head of the patient "like a butterfly," and could simply hand it back to its owner. In more serious cases, he needed to undertake a supernatural journey, in which the retrieved soul was placed within a special "soul-catcher" charm – a carved ivory tube, the ends of which could be stop-

Nootka girls, 1915. Photographed at the village of Hesquiat, this girl is wearing cedar bark ornaments that were tied to the hair of virgins on the fifth morning of their puberty ceremony. These are wrapped with trade cloth decorated with mother of pearl buttons. She also wears a cedar bark cape.

Basketry hat, Nootka, before 1780. The hat carries a depiction of harpoon whale-hunting, an activity for which the Nootka were renowned. This type of decorated hat with a bulb top was worn only by chiefs, who were the only people permitted to wield a harpoon when whaling, and is a very early example.

pered with plugs of cedar bark. But once a soul reached the land of the dead and tasted food there, which was inedible to the living, it was lost.

Coast Salish shamans built "spirit canoes" of painted planking in which such supernatural journeys could be undertaken. The shamans of other areas were thought to journey beneath the seas, where they remained for several hours while they traveled to the abode of the spirits; they would return with blood streaming from their nostrils and muttering words that only they and the spirits could understand.

Every shaman was considered to be simply a body through which a previous shaman exercised his power. Because the previous shaman was similarly linked to a prior existence, the shamanic line could be extended back to ancestral individuals whose voices still spoke. This created a separate lineage of shamans parallel to that of the clans, and it served to distinguish shamans from any other member of the community. Shamans lived separately, beyond the village confines, where they practiced esoteric rituals using knowledge that was denied to others. When they died, their bones were placed in special grave-houses that never decomposed, but which descended slowly and evenly into the ground. Their voices would be heard through younger shamans, but their spirits

Skidegate village, Haida, nineteenth century. This village on the Queen Charlotte Islands was marked by a profusion of totem poles.

Dance apron, Tlingit, 1850–1875. This painted buckskin apron from Cape Fox, Alaska, would have been worn by a shaman, and depicts the supernatural animals by which he was assisted.

Mask, Sitka Tlingit, early nineteenth century. Painted elements suggest clan markings, and the feather forms above the right eye suggest this may have been either the Eagle or Hawk.

▲ Shaman's dolls, Tlingit, nineteenth century. As part of the curing rites and magical performances of Tlingit shamans, small figures were made to appear mysteriously. These figures were puppets, such as those shown here, and were kept in carved and painted wooden boxes together with other shamanic paraphernalia.

▶ Dagger, Tlingit, nineteenth century. The dagger is made from beaten copper with a wooden carved handle wrapped with thread. The animal at the hilt may be either the Wolf or Bear. Such double-edged daggers were used in warfare, so either animal would be appropriate.

would continue to command the coves and inlets – nobody would dare take a canoe through a place that was protected by a shaman's spirit without first casting an offering into the water to guarantee a safe passage.

SOCIAL COMPETITION

The shamans, as well as the dances of the Hamatsa, Dluwulaxa, and Nutlam, were linked to the ancestral powers. All the expressions of Northwest Coast culture, however, were made possible only because their country contained resources that could be gathered in far greater quantities than required for normal consumption. At least six months of the year could be spent in socially competitive events. In these contests the families owning the better salmon-bearing stretches of rivers or berrying fields were at a distinct advantage. The result was a few families engaged in direct rivalry, but supported by numbers of less privileged kin.

During the nineteenth century, European influences and the introduction of trade goods – particularly metal-bladed tools, which made the manufacture of carvings more rapid – increased the number and value of prestige gifts that could be distributed. This led to a situation in which the potlatch started to be used not only to validate a position, but to increase its status by excessive gift-giving.

Because comparable positions were held in each clan, competition developed in attempts to raise the status of a position in one clan above that of the equivalent position in another. Some potlatches were announced as challenges to rival clans. Refusal to accept such a challenge was derided as indicating the rival's inability to give the even greater potlatch that would be needed in the future to elevate one of their own members. The invitation to a potlatch was a declaration of war; but it was a war that would be fought with property rather than with weapons.

Such potlatches required the combined efforts of several clan members to amass the number of gifts required. Insult and ridicule were used in clan leaders' attempts to belittle one another. Great feast bowls were prepared, and the challenged clan was required to eat all they contained. Often one feast would be followed immediately by another. As they ate, the leader of the invited group would bemoan the fact they were being fed so miserably, while his opponent would chide them for having small appetites and eating slowly. Huge piles of gifts were given away and, at times, valuable property might be destroyed, and the pieces flung contemptuously at the feet of the invited group.

Potlatch hat, Tlingit, nineteenth century. Cedar bark rings fasted to the top of this Tlingit spruce-root hat indicate that its wearer had been the sponsor of five potlatches. During dances, the hollow rings were filled with downy eagle feathers, which energetic head movements of the dancer would scatter over the audience.

Basketry hat, Tlingit, nineteenth century. This hat is typical of the north and northwest coasts and displays the Tlingit preference for keeping design elements to the upper sector and allowing the lower half to show pattern in the weave. The painting on the upper part depicts the Eagle, which was an important Tlingit clan totem.

EXTREME COMPETITION

At its height, the escalation involved in the competition potlatch, especially among the Kwakiutl, meant the production of goods could not keep up with their distribution. Objects were assigned a value according to how many Hudson Bay trade blankets they were worth. Tally-sticks, which had predetermined blanket values, were frequently used instead of actual goods.

More important were plaques beaten from native copper (and later from trade copper) that had been traded into the area. These had high initial values, which increased each time they were used: a copper worth, say, 1,000 blankets at its first potlatch could be worth 2,000 at the next. Coppers could even be partially distributed by being cut into sections. If the pieces were potlatched to separate clans, they gained value rapidly. But it was also possible to challenge each of the groups to obtain the pieces and rivet them back together. A restored copper had a value based on all the potlatches at which it had featured, and this could run into thousands of blankets.

The competition potlatches were great social events. Although people would always remember the name of a leader whose clan had sponsored one, there were a number of visible indicators of achievement in use as well. Among the Tlingit, potlatch hats were adorned with hollow cedar bark rings. A new ring would be added for each potlatch to serve as constant reminders of the wearer's greatness. Wooden carvings of a figure holding a copper plaque were placed before houses in which a copper had been displayed, and the house was said to "groan under the copper's weight." The Haida demonstrated the strength of their clans with beautifully carved portrait masks, which displayed a sequence explaining the powers with which the clan and family lineage was associated.

THE STABILITY OF THE PAST

Despite the high drama and exuberant detail of the dances and potlatches, there was a static element in Northwest Coast culture that resisted change and innovation. The ranked positions were finite in number and could only be aspired to by particular individuals. Dances, though they might be extreme, were nevertheless predictable and carefully stage-managed. Shamanic activity followed a very specific set of ritual formulas. Carvings had a strict formal order that permitted no deviation, so that an early mask and a recent one employ identical forms and details. All of these were part of a long line that fastened Northwest Coast culture securely to a past that was hidden in the fogs and mists of the coast.

CHAPTER FIVE

The Forest Dwellers

and surrounded by embankments and ditches in complex geometric configurations.

The mounds were both honorific monuments and a means of asserting authority over the environment. Eventually they took on new shapes as realistic figures that may have served as clan markers. The most famous is the Great Serpent Mound, which twists and coils along the top of an exposed hillside in Ohio for a distance of 1,300 ft (400m). It is a magnificent representation of a people's ability to draw strength from the earth. To create such a mound required a stupendous effort, since earth had to be carried by the basket-load. A similar industriousness marks everything the Adena-Hopewell people did. They established communities as far afield as the lower Mississippi, Kansas, and upper New York State, although Ohio was to remain the center of their culture. They built earlier exchange routes into a great trade network that virtually spanned the continent.

Silver was imported from Ontario, obsidian from the Rocky Mountains, grizzly bear teeth from Wyoming, and shells from the Gulf Coast. All of these materials were worked into exquisitely carved and incised objects, which were often intended purely as grave goods to accompany the deceased. Sheet mica and copper were used in making cutouts of serpents

FORESTS FILLED THE area east of the Mississippi River, from the Subarctic of the north and thence south into Florida. These were far from being uniform, ranging from pine in the relatively cold north to tropical swamp cypress and mangrove in Florida, with deciduous and mixed forest in between. All, however, evoke a sense of permanence and offer shade and protection for plant and animal life, as well as to the human populations that lived here. The forests have a quality of stillness and peace, but this can be illusory, for they may hide dangers.

People living in such environments have evolved a number of strategies for dealing with the inherent dangers: by enlisting the help of benign local forces; by the formation of large communities, where activities can be carried out by groups rather than individuals; and by physically altering the environment to provide greater security at both the physical and spiritual levels.

THE ADENA-HOPEWELL

There had been a number of early societies in this area, going back some 5,000 to 7,000 years ago with the Red Paint and Old Copper cultures. These people had developed complex hierarchies and elaborate technology, indicating that they were using at least two of the strategies above – communal activity and physical intervention. It is, however, with the Adena-Hopewell people, who flourished from about 3,000 years ago until 800 A.D., that the basic cultural institutions were founded on which later developments would be built. In southern Ohio and parts of West Virginia, Pennsylvania, Kentucky, and Indiana, the Adena-Hopewell began honoring prominent members of their groups by piling earth over tombs to form low mounds. Later the mounds were increased in size

Sheet mica cut-out, Adena-Hopewell, c100B.C. – 500A.D. The Adena-Hopewell imported sheet mica from the southern Appalachians and fashioned it into shapes representing human hands, animal and bird figures, and talons, or serpents such as that shown here. These may have had cult or clan significance.

Deer mask, Mound Spiro, Oklahoma, c1000A.D. This elaborate mask is carved from a single block of cedar and has mouth and eyes (and formerly also ears) inlaid with shell. It may have been worn by a shaman during the Deer Ceremony that was intended to bring game within easy reach of the hunters.

Bandoleer bag, Delaware. This Delaware bandoleer pouch combines indigenous materials with those introduced by European colonists. The bag is of buckskin and has a traditional wide strap that was worn across the chest, but the decoration is in beads, wool tassels, and colored cloth strips.

LOCATIONS OF THE EASTERN WOODLANDS INDIANS

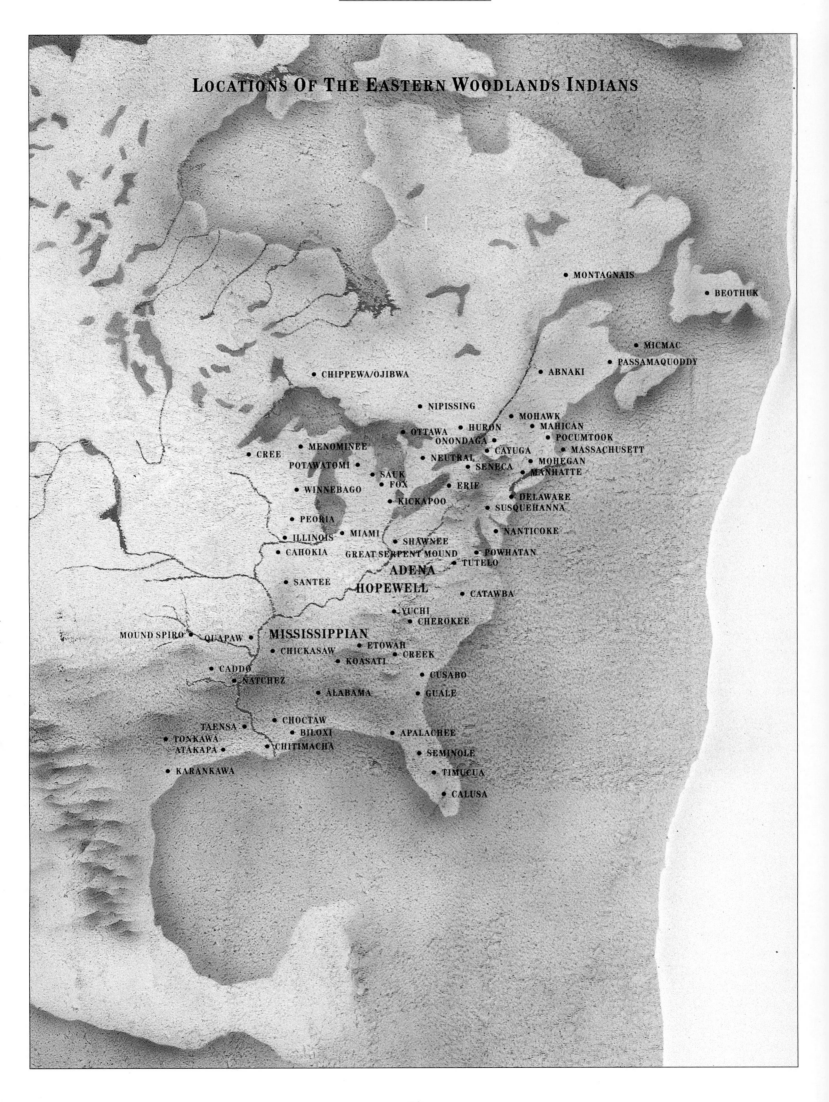

• MONTAGNAIS

• BEOTHUK

• MICMAC
• PASSAMAQUODDY

• CHIPPEWA/OJIBWA
• ABNAKI

• NIPISSING
• MOHAWK
• OTTAWA HURON • MAHICAN
ONONDAGA • POCUMTOOK
• MENOMINEE NEUTRAL • CAYUGA • MASSACHUSETT
• CREE SENECA • MOHEGAN
POTAWATOMI • SAUK • MANHATTE
• FOX ERIE
• WINNEBAGO • DELAWARE
• KICKAPOO • SUSQUEHANNA

• PEORIA • NANTICOKE
• MIAMI
• ILLINOIS • SHAWNEE • POWHATAN
• CAHOKIA GREAT SERPENT MOUND • TUTELO
ADENA
• SANTEE **HOPEWELL** • CATAWBA

• YUCHI
• CHEROKEE
MOUND SPIRO **MISSISSIPPIAN**
• QUAPAW • ETOWAH
• CHICKASAW • CREEK
• KOASATI
• CADDO • CUSABO
• NATCHEZ
• ALABAMA • GUALE
TAENSA • CHOCTAW
TONKAWA • BILOXI • APALACHEE
ATAKAPA • CHITIMACHA
• SEMINOLE
• KARANKAWA
• TIMUCUA
• CALUSA

and eagles, but perhaps the high point of their art was the manufacture of tubular pipes depicting benign animal spirits. These pipes are amazingly life-like and beautifully carved, reflecting an acute understanding of animal behavior. They indicate the probable origin of smoking rituals that were later to spread right across the North American continent, when they were used to promote general feelings of peace, friendship, and truth.

THE MISSISSIPPIANS

Adena-Hopewell influence was far-reaching, but between 400 and 600 A.D., it started to decline and cleared the way for a new development further to the south. This was the Mississippian culture, which would continue into the historic period with the Natchez and Taensa. The Mississippians took over many of the existing Adena-Hopewell cultural traits, including ranked chieftainship, agriculture, and the erecting of earth mounds. An aggressive element, however, was present in their culture. The exalted leader became a demigod, and the earth mound a flat-topped pyramid in which an eternal fire was kept burning. Farmers and traders were now warriors, members of fighting élites that were aggressively expanding their territories as part of a politico-religious movement known as the Southern Death Cult. They subjugated neighboring tribes, who were forced to pay tribute.

Villages grew in size to become city-states containing thousands of people, and the earthworks became bigger. Cahokia, in Illinois, occupies an area of over 5 square miles (13 square kilometers) and has almost 100 mounds (the largest, Monk's Mound, has a volume exceeding that of the Great Pyramid in Egypt). The rapid expansion of the Mississippians was possible only through the development of a new strain of corn that matured quickly and provided two harvests a year. It is significant that the western limit of expansion was in the area of the Caddo-Mississippians at Mound Spiro, Oklahoma, beyond which the new corn would not mature.

THE NATCHEZ

The heyday of the Mississippian cults was over by the time De Soto arrived in 1540. Many of their beliefs, however, were still being expressed by tribes such as the Natchez, who were living in several fortified villages in the lower Mississippi Valley. These villages consisted of a number of rectangular mud-plastered houses with curved roofs of bent saplings covered with thatch. The houses were built around a mound supporting a wooden temple that contained the bones of previous chiefs. Natchez chiefs, known as Great

Suns, were despotic leaders with absolute rule over their people. This rule was inherited through the mother – descent was reckoned matriarchally – and was believed to be sanctioned by the deities, of whom the Great Sun was the personification on earth.

EARLY FLORIDA TRIBES

The only immediate neighbors of the Mississippians not to be directly influenced by them were the Florida tribes: the Apalachee, Timucua, and Calusa. They, too, were warlike peoples. When the Spanish galleons

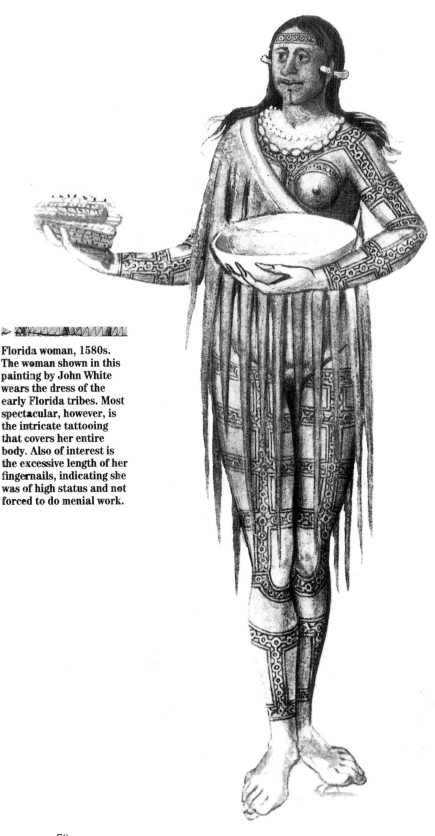

Florida woman, 1580s. The woman shown in this painting by John White wears the dress of the early Florida tribes. Most spectacular, however, is the intricate tattooing that covers her entire body. Also of interest is the excessive length of her fingernails, indicating she was of high status and not forced to do menial work.

of Ponce de Leon arrived in 1513, they were driven off by the war canoes of the Calusa. These tribes do not appear to have been expansionist, however, probably because there was little need to compete for resources in Florida, the "flourishing land," where food was available in sufficient quantities to support a relatively large population.

The Florida tribes were river dwellers and sea-farers, subsisting largely on fish and shellfish, but they also hunted deer, birds, and reptiles of various kinds. Even the alligator was hunted for its meat and skin. Spanish reports describe the people as spectacu-

Carved marble figures, Etowah, Georgia, c1400–1500A.D. Although several similar seated figures have been found in log tombs from this period, little is known about them. They may be portraits of ancestors, or could represent cult figures.

larly tattooed. They wore little clothing because it was unnecessary in this tropical climate. The men wore only a breechcloth and the women an apron of bluish-green tree moss woven into intricate patterns, and adorned with myriads of irridescent sea shells. Both sexes wore a profusion of necklaces and earrings of shells, bone, and seeds.

Unfortunately, very little is known about the culture of these early Floridians. Spanish and French attempts to missionize them met with little success. But the missions introduced diseases to which the tribes had little resistance, and the weakened groups fell easy prey to the British who, with Indian allies, invaded their territories in the mid-1700s. The tribes were destroyed and the remnants enslaved or deported to Cuba.

THE FIVE CIVILIZED TRIBES

Modern Florida Indians are the Seminole. Unrelated to the original inhabitants, they are a refugee group composed mainly of Creek and African-American blood who fled into the depths of the Everglades in an attempt to escape oppression from the first unions of settlers. Here they erected open-sided, palmetto-thatched lodges, raised on stilts to keep them above the level of the marshland waters. Their culture, like that of the Creek, is essentially a hybrid one dependent on many different influences.

The Creek and Seminole, together with the Chero-kee, Choctaw, and Chickasaw, living farther to the north in the swamplands that centered on the Carol-

Baskets, Chitimacha/Cherokee. Such split-cane baskets reflect the brilliance of tropical forests in their use of color. Colonel Nicholson, Governor of South Carolina, described them as ". . . made by the Indians of Splitt Canes some parts of them being dyed red . . . and black. They will keep anything in them from being wetted by rain."

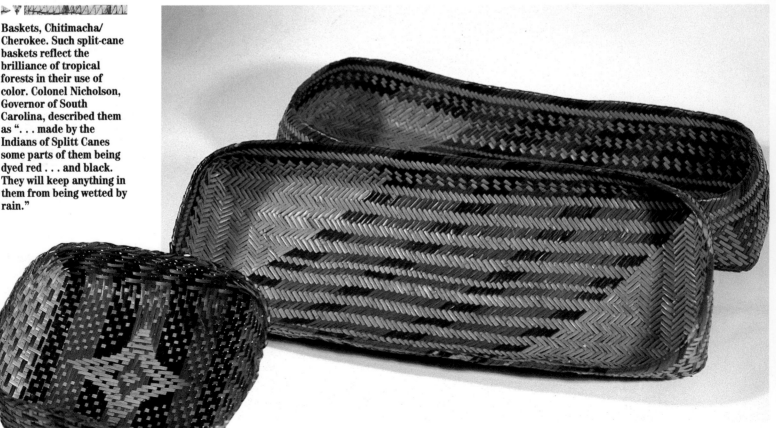

inas, are known collectively as "The Five Civilized Tribes." They had social systems based on concepts of individual ownership and established institutions comparable with the schools and law courts of the first settlers. They were quick to adopt stock-raising and to abandon much of their traditional dress for European clothing. All this, in the view of the European settlers, marked them out as more "civilized" than other tribes of the area.

All these people were, essentially, farmers. Individual ownership of land, however, meant that a moneyed aristocracy came into being, and a few individuals had disproportionate influence in the

Palmetto house, Choctaw. Such housing reflects the semi-tropical nature of the southern Woodlands environments in the materials used for construction. This house is thatched with palmetto leaves. Palmetto is a species of fan palm native to southeastern areas.

debates of the town councils. The result was factionalism and bitter inter-family feuding. This came to a head in 1815 with the Creek Civil War, when pro- and anti-American factions clashed head-on, splitting the tribe and creating the anti-American refugees who formed the Seminole. The victorious pro-Americans had little time to enjoy their success. Settlers clamored for the rich agricultural lands they occupied. Calls for the removal of the Five Civilized Tribes led, in 1825, to the start of the infamous "Trails of Tears." The Indians were forced to march, often in manacles, to their new "homeland" in Indian Territory (Oklahoma) so that their lands could be settled.

Village scene, Delaware. When the Spanish first entered the Woodlands areas, they found the people living in fortified villages with small plots of ground cleared for growing crops. This early engraving shows a Delaware village, which is of a type of construction similar to that used by other tribes of the region.

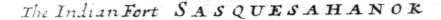

The Indian Fort SASQUESAHANOK

Creek man. As in the picture of No English, this man has taken over European dress to some extent, but the fur shoulder strap, bird wing fan, and fingerwoven headband are all traditional items.

Seminole women. Refugees from the Creek tribes fled into the Florida Everglades after the confederacy was broken. Here they joined with the remnants of other tribes to create the Seminole. The women here wear the highly characteristic patchwork dresses of this tribe.

82

●●●

No-English, Peoria, 1830.
No-English was mentioned
by George Catlin, who
took this photograph, as
being a "beau" who took
great care over his
appearance. The
photograph shows the
influence of European
styles of dress that was
apparent throughout the
Woodlands areas from an
early date.

Shoulder bag, Creek,
nineteenth century. This
small shoulder bag shows
the characteristic massed
forms of Creek beadwork.
Beads were obtained in
trade, and the Creek were
influenced at an early
date by European
colonists. It is assumed,
however, that something
of earlier motifs remains
in such beadwork.

Small pouch, Huron, eighteenth century. The pouch is woven from hemp, and has embroidered moosehair decoration. Larger bags of a similar type, but with a shoulder strap, were used for carrying shot for trade muskets. The size of this bag suggests that it contained personal items and would have been worn tucked into a belt or sash.

Woven sash, Huron, c1830. This fingerwoven-yarn sash is an exquisite example of Iroquois artistry. The five-banded design contains trade beads that have been woven in near the points of the arrowheads. Similar beads are also braided into the fringes.

Ball-headed war club, Ojibwa, nineteenth century. Ball-headed war clubs were widely distributed throughout the Woodlands and even among some of the Plains tribes. This example is made from wood and has a small mammal figure, possibly an otter, carved on the back.

Sa Ga Yeath Qua Pieth Tow, Iroquois, 1710. Sa Ga Yeath Qua Pieth Tow was a Mohawk Sachem, or chief, and one of a group of Mohawk men who visited Queen Anne in London, England, in 1710. The designs on his face and body are tattoos, and, although his costume is romanticized, it is still possible to detect traditional dress items.

THE IROQUOIS

The east coastal regions were home to Algonquian- and Iroquoian-speaking tribes. Although the Iroquois were ancient inhabitants of the Woodlands, they had moved north from their original lands to force the Algonquins further to the east and onto the coasts. Like other occupants of the forest lands, they were corn farmers who cleared forest patches for their fields and built permanent villages. The Iroquois, however, gained a reputation for efficient ruthlessness. As a result of continual warfare, both among themselves and with other tribes of the region, they were forced to erect protective palisades around their villages of characteristic elmbark longhouses. The villages were concentrated primarily in the Valley of the Mohawk.

Households were owned and administered by women, matriarchs of the tribes, and everything a man did he reported back to the Clan Mother of his wife's family. Clan Mothers were powerful, controlling and directing all aspects of Iroquois life in both the domestic and political spheres. They decided who would be selected from among the men to represent the people as their spokesman and when crops would be planted and harvested. On marriage, a man moved in with and supported his wife's grandmother, mother, and the families of her sisters.

THE LEAGUE OF FIVE NATIONS

The men were, first and foremost, warriors; but continuous warfare seriously weakened the tribes. A reformer, known to us as Hiawatha, proposed a league of nations in which the Iroquois could act in concert against any threat to themselves, but would not fight with one another. His ideas met with scepticism and resistance, but through stubborn determination he eventually persuaded five of the tribes to form a confederacy. A formal "document" was drawn up on a wampum belt. White and purple beads were used to make a permanent record of the agreement they had reached. The completed belt was deposited in the safekeeping of the Onondaga, the Keepers of the Central Council Fire.

The League of Five Nations, comprising the Seneca, Cayuga, Onondaga, Oneida, and Mohawk, consisted of independent tribes who agreed to act cooperatively in matters of attack and defense. Each tribe would cast a vote to decide on what action should be taken. Later, in 1715, a sixth tribe, The Tuscarora, was admitted to the League – although they never voted and had their interests represented by the Oneida. Other Iroquois tribes held back from joining. The Huron had already formed a confederacy of their own, and the Tobacco – who are often referred to as the

Burden straps, Iroquois, 1710. Burden straps, or tumplines, were used when carrying heavy loads. The ends of the straps were tied about the load to be carried and the broad band was passed across the forehead or chest. The undecorated strap is woven from vegetable fiber. The other is hemp decorated with moosehair embroidery.

Cord, probably Iroquois, eighteenth or nineteenth century. Likely to have been used for any number of different purposes, this cord is made from braided vegetable fiber and decorated with porcupine quills and tin cone dangles containing dyed hair.

Neutrals – preferred to stay separate and totally independent. Both these groups fell victim to Five Nations retaliation: the Huron because of their open defiance of the League, and the Neutrals because they gave refugee Hurons sanctuary and refused to hand them over.

Although with hindsight the League of Nations appears to have encouraged the notion of gain for a select unified group, it nevertheless impressed the early colonists. In 1744, when the States of Connecticut and Pennsylvania negotiated with the Iroquois to adjust land claims, the constitution of the Five Nations was written into the States' laws. Later, with the establishment of the Federalist Party in 1789, the constitution of the League became enshrined in the Constitution of the United States.

Hunting bag, Shawnee, early nineteenth century. Made from dark dyed leather, this bag is decorated with porcupine quills and tin cone dangles containing red-dyed deer hair. The strap is trimmed with black silk.

Plaited bag, Ojibwa, before 1868. This large Ojibwa checkerweave bag uses the natural pattern of bark to create visual interest. It is woven from the inner bark of the white cedar.

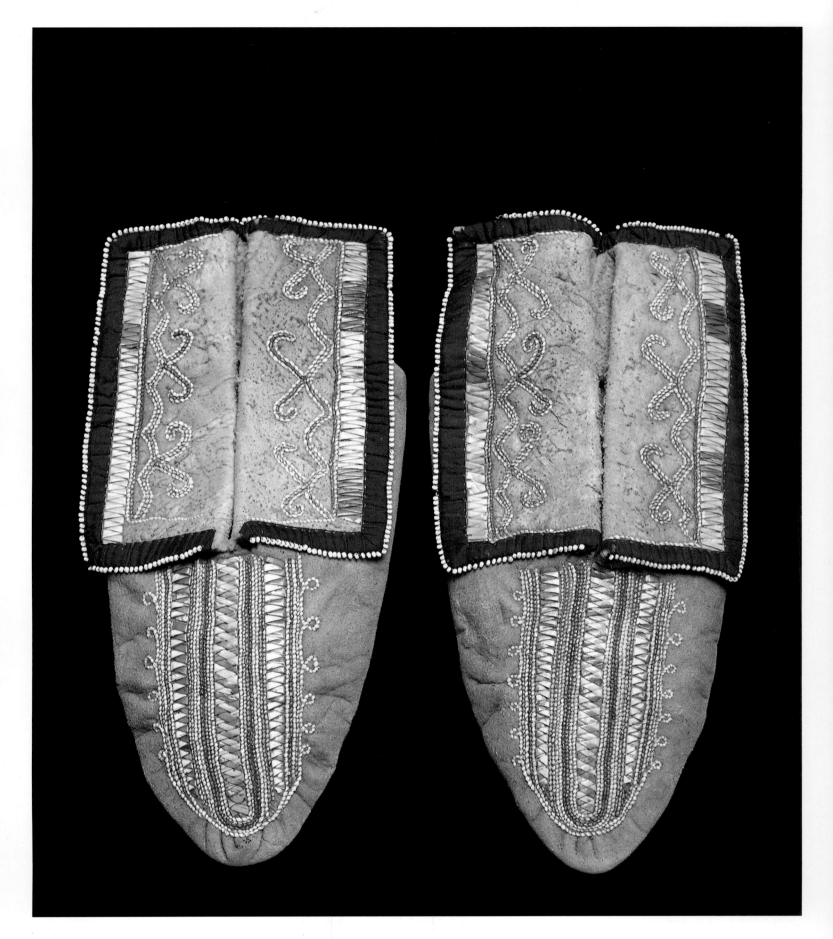

Moccasins, Iroquois, late
nineteenth century. These
moccasins have beads and
cloth applied to smoked
deerskin. The beads and
cloth on the flaps are
trade goods which,
together with porcupine
quills, create a style
formerly produced solely
with quills.

COOPERATION AND HARMONY

Iroquois aggression needs to be understood in light of the fact that the Algonquin territories they moved into were not known for their peace and tranquillity. If they had not fought harder and more successfully than their adversaries, they would have been unable to survive.

Within their households, the Iroquois demonstrate a great deal of cooperative sharing and support. Disputes were settled by arbitration, children were rarely punished, and even captives were accorded the same respect as any other member of the community (with the single exception that they had no vote in the council deliberations). Fields of corn and tobacco were owned and managed jointly, and the longhouse was a symbol of communal sharing in which families worked together in preparing meals and caring for children.

Even their conception of the spiritual world leaves no room for evil. It is based on the idea of struggles between opposing dualities such as light and dark, or good and misfortune, in which there is an essential harmony. It was only when something happened to disturb the balance that ceremonies were needed to bring things back into order. Ceremonies were the responsibility of secret societies, of which the Iroquois had many. The best known is that of the False Faces, whose dancers wore masks bearing exaggerated features, which had been carved on a living tree. The connection with hidden local resources is evident. The mask became the embodiment of the soul inherent in the tree from which it had been carved, and thus it made the soul visible so that it could be released and utilized in the people's world.

THE ALGONQUIN

Although the Iroquois managed to establish themselves as the dominant force in the New York State area, Algonquian-speakers had strong alliances of their own and controlled the entire coastal region from North Carolina through Virginia, Maryland, Delaware, New Jersey, New England, and into Maine. Although they lived on or near the coasts, they looked inward to the forests rather than out to the sea, and made little use of marine resources other than shellfish. They relied on the products of their fields and on woodland animals and plants. Formal confederacies, such as those of the Iroquois, were not made. Instead, several small groups allied themselves in pacts of friendship within which each group was able to act independently when occasion arose.

Some of these alliances were more stable than others; one of the more successful was that of some 200 villages from 30 different tribes held together

Yarn bag, possibly Huron. A finger-woven bag in which the patterns derive from beads that have been interwoven with the yarn strands.

Garter drops, possibly Iroquois. These would orginally have been sewn into a pair of garters so that they hung suspended along the outer side of the leg. They are made from bead-decorated finger-woven yarn, which has been resist dyed leaving uncolored bands.

Garters, possibly Iroquois. Made of dyed wool or hair, and decorated with white beads and long quillwork cords, ending in hair tassels, these garters were worn tied around the leg, just below the knee.

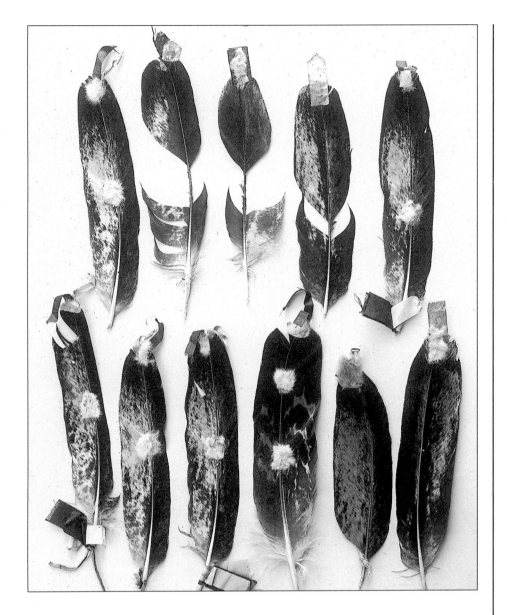

modern usage to refer to any gathering of American Indians from different tribes. Powwows were occasions of feasting and gift giving, accompanied by singing, dancing, gambling, and contests of skill. Contrary to the similar gatherings of tribes in other areas, those of the Algonquins do not seem to have placed any emphasis on a ritual or ceremonial aspect. Powwows were devoted exclusively to the establishment of friendly relationships.

This, perhaps, is to be expected. The forest environment suggests that influential forces would have been local rather than ones affecting a disparate group drawn together from great distances. Similarities existed between groups, of course, for even widely separated tribes occupied essentially the same country. The differences were great enough, however, for each tribe to consider chiefly those elements of immediate relevance to the survival of their particular community, and this was not conducive to tribal celebration. There was a need to join together in friendship, but not to collaborate in ceremonies or to invoke the same spiritual powers.

A particular class of artifact, the friendship bag, reflects the nature of the powwow. These shoulder pouches were beautifully made and richly embellished with elaborate patterns made from the thread of the inner bark of swamp ash, or of deerskin decorated with porcupine quills. They were exclusively reserved to be packed with meat or other gifts and presented as gestures of friendship and goodwill. A man setting off for a powwow would carry several of these pouches with him, which he would give to people whom he had befriended on previous occasions.

EARLY EUROPEAN CONTACT

Algonquian Indians were among the first of the Woodland tribes to encounter European colonists. Powhatan's confederacy made it possible for the British to establish Jamestown in 1607. For the first years of its existence, Jamestown was totally dependent on supplies procured for it by the Indians. The Powhatan were also, unfortunately, the first to be abused by the colonists. In 1622 and 1644, the confederacy was shattered by the British; and in 1676, the few remaining refugees were massacred by Virginia settlers. Other groups in this area suffered similar depredations at the hands of the French.

It was common policy for both the British and French to enlist Indian allies and to set tribes with traditional enmities against each other. This seriously weakened many of the groups and undermined the traditional leadership roles, which were usurped by the colonists and left the groups open to military exploitation. Many groups lost their viability as tribal entities in this manner. Others, unable to respond

under the leadership of Powhatan. Many Algonquian alliances, however, were frequently undermined by petty feuding and squabbles. These were generally family affairs and rivalries, prosecuted through ambushes in which one or two people might be killed. But they made the creation of permanent confederacies difficult because there would always be somebody who bore a grudge against another. Villages were therefore small, with garden plots rather than the fields of the confederated tribes. They lacked the highly organized structure of the towns found among tribes such as the Creek. The main characteristics the Algonquins shared with other tribes of the region were the cultivation of corn and respect for their chiefs, or Werowances, whose remains were preserved in a building tended by a special caste of priests.

POWWOWS

Algonquian life was generally peaceful. They could defend themselves effectively when necessary, but preferred to settle matters at a tribal level through overtures of peace and gift-giving. Central to this was the idea of the powwow – a term that has come into

War honor feathers, Chippewa. Status and honor acquired through war exploits was publicly displayed. One method was to wear eagle feathers, cut in different ways to depict specific war exploits, such as rescuing a fallen comrade or covering a retreat. The meanings of the feather cuts in this photograph are not recorded.

Male-Caribou, Chippewa, 1836. Male Caribou, painted by George Caitlin, seems to have been little influenced by European tastes, and retains his native dress and body decoration. He wears a fingerwoven sash as a turban and carries a "gunstock" war club.

War club, 1820. The "gunstock" type of war club was used throughout the Woodlands, and as far west as the Mississippi-Missouri. The steel blade is inset into a carved and painted wood handle that is wrapped with snakeskin.

effectively to the pressures being exerted on them, fled west and left the area entirely.

LIFE BY THE GREAT LAKES

The only Algonquins to escape the brunt of the British-French conflict were those living in the region of the Great Lakes, such as the Chippewa. Too far north for successful large-scale agriculture, they occupied lands that were beautiful, but which held little interest for the European settlers. Their lives were similar to those of the other Algonquins of the region, except for a dependence on wild rice as a staple

instead of corn. Great expanses of rice grew in the shallow waters at the edges of the lakes. It was an easy matter to maneuver a birchbark canoe among the rice. By bending the plants over a stretched hide and beating them with a stick, it was a simple matter to obtain considerable quantities of rice. Wild birds, particularly ducks, were readily available and could be lured into traps with decoys made from wood and rush. The woods teemed with moose and deer.

The lives of these people was comfortable, but the northern areas imbued them with a sense of elements that were to be feared and respected. Carved wooden posts bearing ancestral figures were erected around

Moccasins. Smoked to darker their color, these moccasins are decorated with porcupine quills, beads, and hair-filled tin cones. They are of a high-sided style worn by several woodland tribes in the Great Lakes region.

the villages to turn away any negative influence that sought entry. These figures represented the animate soul that the Chippewa believed existed in every aspect of their world. This soul went back to ancient forces more powerful than those of the present.

It was also believed that everything had an identity that could be linked with the identity of the people; all things were created simultaneously and none took precedence. When fishing, these Algonquins never returned twice in succession to the same lake, nor would they tap a maple tree to secure sugar two years in a row. The lake and the tree had given themselves willingly, and it was a sign of respect to leave them in peace and allow time for their recovery.

The Chippewa created a great ceremonial institution called the Midéwiwin, the Grand Medicine Lodge or Mystic Society of Animals – which referred to the mysterious world in which people and animals conversed in a common tongue and where the reasons for existence could be affirmed. Through these ceremonies, they, and their allies in the Three Fires Confederacy, the Ottawa and Potawatomi, could con-

tinually restate the close links between the worlds of the people and the animals. The ceremony united them as one and emphasized the fact that they existed equally and for mutual benefit.

ALLIANCES THAT NEVER CAME

It is impossible to guess what the future would have held for the Woodlands had it not been for the devastating effect on their cultures of European incursions. It is likely they would have formed stronger confederacies, such as that of the Five Nations. They would have been very dependent on agricultural produce, however, and could only have been achieved by physically altering the land and clearing forest areas for fields. It is significant that the most elaborate rituals for dealing with the unknown forces of the country were those of the Chippewa, living too far north for extensive farming and dependent solely on what nature provided. It is also among these people that we find the least aggressive expressions of the region.

CHAPTER SIX

The Far West

THE FAR WEST contains three distinct culture regions edging onto the Pacific Ocean; those of California, the Desert West, and the Plateau. California corresponds almost exactly to the modern state; the Desert West is, essentially, the Great Basin of Utah, Nevada, and southern Oregon; the Plateau lies north of this in parts of Idaho, Washington state, and inland British Columbia, in the area drained by the Fraser and Columbia rivers.

CALIFORNIA

California has many different environments: redwood and sequoia forests, containing the world's largest and oldest trees, are found in the northern parts; oak parkland dominates the central areas; the south is scrub chaparral. Throughout the region there is a generally warm, Mediterranean climate, which attracted a high aboriginal population. Estimates are that there were originally as many as 500 separate tribal groups speaking at least 100 different languages.

Who these people were and what their lives were like is largely a matter of surmise and guesswork. The Spanish sailor, Cabrillo, sailed along their coast in 1542, and various other Spaniards visited the area infrequently over the next 200 years. They all viewed the California Indians as relics of a bygone age and took no interest in recording their customs and lifestyles. When the Spanish began to establish missions in 1769, they herded together people who happened to be living nearby, with no regard for tribal affiliation, language, or custom. These people had no cultural response for aggression; warfare was not a part of their lives, and they possessed no weapons for either defense or attack. They proved submissive and easy prey to Spanish domination.

The Spanish presence extended as far as what is now San Francisco, although few Spaniards actually chose to live in the area. For a short period the Treaty of Guadalupe-Hidalgo, made in 1821, put California in Mexican hands. This period was too brief for the Mexicans to cause any further damage, because the United States wrested control during the Mexican War of 1846. In 1848, however, the California Gold Rush began, flooding the area with Protestant gold-seekers. Their Puritan ethic prevented them from considering any other belief framework. To them, the Indians were simply a nuisance that happened to be in the way. Many Indians were killed and others enslaved. Within ten years, all the tribes of southern and central California had ceased to exist as viable tribal entities.

We are now left only with a "memory" of cultures that must have been among the gentlest and most amiable ever known. All we can do is pick through the scanty early records and clutch at fragments told

by elders around the turn of the century, who remembered something of what their grandparents and great-grandparents had told them about a way of life that they themselves had never known.

STABILITY AND TRADITION

The early Spanish reports describe the lives of the Californians as "sparse." The tribes did not have elaborate social institutions and ceremonies, nor did they practice agriculture or build great houses and

Seri girl, 1894. Although living in Mexico, the Seri are part of the Californian culture area. Candelaria, an unmarried girl, was photographed in Sonora. The face-painting denotes her family. Among the Seri, only the women wore painted designs, with the occasional exception of very young boys.

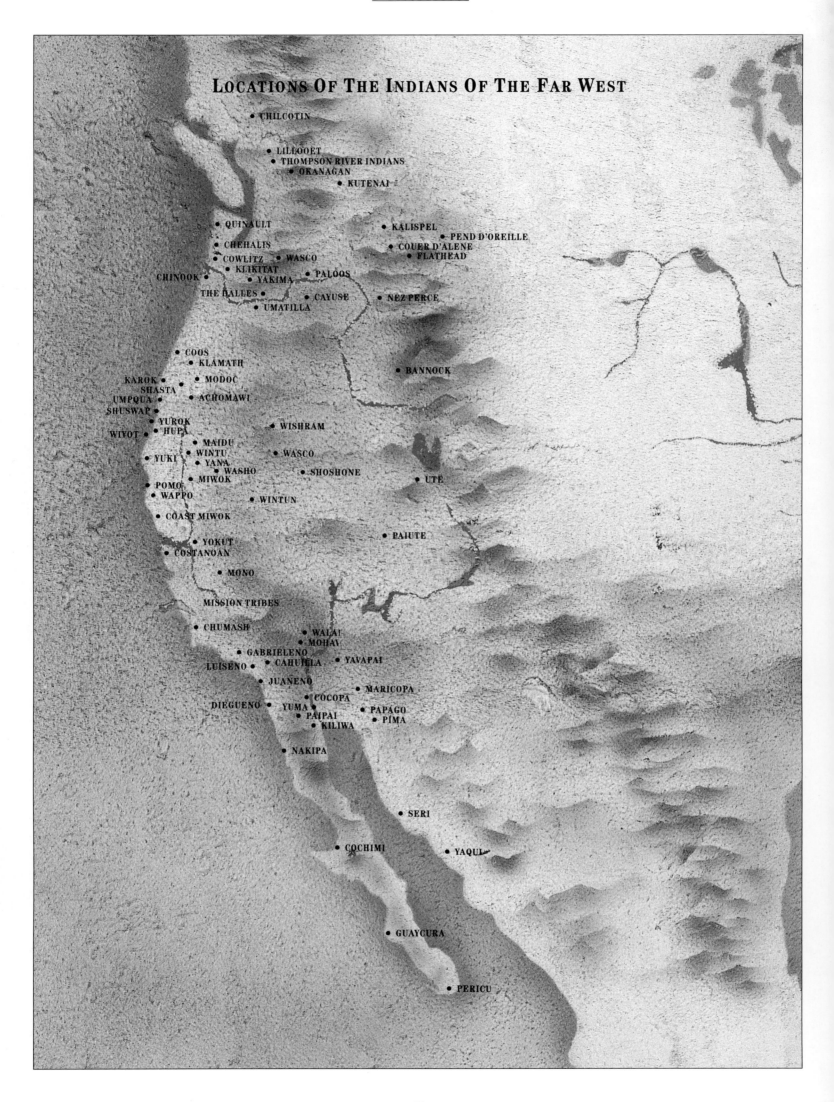

LOCATIONS OF THE INDIANS OF THE FAR WEST

- CHILCOTIN
- LILLOOET
- THOMPSON RIVER INDIANS
- OKANAGAN
- KUTENAI
- QUINAULT
- KALISPEL
- PEND D'OREILLE
- CHEHALIS
- COUER D'ALENE
- COWLITZ
- WASCO
- FLATHEAD
- KLIKITAT
- PALOOS
- CHINOOK
- YAKIMA
- THE DALLES
- CAYUSE
- NEZ PERCE
- UMATILLA
- COOS
- KLAMATH
- BANNOCK
- KAROK
- MODOC
- SHASTA
- UMPQUA
- ACHOMAWI
- SHUSWAP
- YUROK
- WISHRAM
- WIYOT
- HUPA
- MAIDU
- WINTU
- WASCO
- YUKI
- YANA
- WASHO
- SHOSHONE
- POMO
- MIWOK
- UTE
- WAPPO
- WINTUN
- COAST MIWOK
- PAIUTE
- YOKUT
- COSTANOAN
- MONO
- MISSION TRIBES
- CHUMASH
- WALAI
- MOHAV
- GABRIELENO
- LUISENO
- CAHUILLA
- YAVAPAI
- JUANENO
- MARICOPA
- COCOPA
- DIEGUENO
- YUMA
- PAPAGO
- PAIPAI
- PIMA
- KILIWA
- NAKIPA
- SERI
- COCHIMI
- YAQUI
- GUAYCURA
- PERICU

LOCATIONS OF THE INDIANS OF THE FAR WEST

Hair ornament, Northern California, 1790–35. Similar to others that are credited to the Hupa, this ornament would have been worn by a person of high status. It is made from pieces of abalone shell and quartz, which have been fastened to leather strips wrapped with vegetable fiber.

Shell string, Northern California, 1790–95. This string of abalone is of a type known as kaia, which was used as currency when trading and as a symbol of wealth. Such strings were worn by women as necklaces and bracelets, or were sewn onto clothing. The shell pieces here have been shaped and pierced for stringing on a leather thong.

Necklace, nineteenth century. Although this necklace probably came from the Northwest Coast, it is almost identical to ones from central and northern California. The abalone used is Californian, but the beads are of a type introduced to the area by the first European explorers.

monuments. Yet, from the little we know, it is obvious that Californian life was based on stability and continuity, not on ostentatious display. There was little need to develop farming because their country had resources that could be easily gathered. Myths indicated no desire to embrace innovation. The people were perfectly content with their world, and the tales state quite firmly that they originated in the areas where they still lived. Their way of life had been laid down by the ancients. Californian lifestyles were rooted in effective ways of utilizing their resources, and this was based on experience and tradition.

Hunting-gathering and fishing economies seem to have been typical, varying according to the locality in which the people were living. Mussels, abalone, salmon, and small sea mammals were important among the tribes of the coastal areas. Seeds, berries, tubers, roots, nuts, fruits, and bulbs dominated the economies of the inland tribes. The acorn was virtually a staple food for some tribes, collected in the oak parklands or traded with other groups. All these diets

were supplemented by small game and wildfowl.

The Californians' contentment and character were noted by Sebastian Vizcaino when he came to the area in 1602. He described the people as the friendliest on earth. He was amazed at the strength of the men, who would walk with a load that a Spaniard could barely lift, and wrote glowingly of the women, describing them as the comeliest and most beautifully proportioned he had ever encountered. Vizcaino's reports emphasize the mildness and courtesy, reluctance to cause annoyance, and the shyness of the central Californian tribes such as the Pomo, Miwok, Maidu, Wintu, Wintun, Mono, and Mariposa.

Elsewhere we find comments on their relaxed and easy mode of speech and movement, and about their villages in which earth- or mat-covered lodges commonly surrounded a larger, open-sided, men's meeting house. These villages were established within well defined tribal boundaries, under the leadership of a local chief, or Big Man. Some of the Big Men were influential in their own communities, but we find no indication anywhere to suggest they ever attempted to exert authority beyond the territory of the local group. These were small, stable, uncompetitive worlds in which everyone seems to have coexisted peacefully, exchanging and trading local specialty products with other tribes. Shells were traded from the coast to the inland; obsidian, flint, salt, furs, and wood found their way from the hills into the valleys; and the valley tribes traded back acorns to the peoples of the coasts and hills.

A Land of Plenty

The Elders told us there was never a need to fear shortages or famine, nor for the men to spend long periods away from the villages hunting. Much time was spent in the meeting house, which was the focus of the men's social life. They slept and ate here, prepared the items needed for their rituals, and gave quiet instruction to young boys about tribal traditions. Women devoted much of their time to making baskets. Some of these were tiny miniatures with stitches so fine that they are difficult to distinguish with the naked eye, and which were made purely as demonstrations of skill. They also made great storage baskets, as tall as a man, in which acorns could be kept. A basket this large might take a year to make, yet the weave and pattern would remain perfectly consistent. Other baskets used for cooking were woven so tightly they were waterproof.

Not content with simply using different colored reeds and grasses to create patterns, many Californian baskets are decorated with shells and beads, or a pattern is established through variations in the weave itself. Perhaps the most beautiful of all were the gift-baskets of the Pomo. These have brilliant feathers of meadowlarks, hummingbirds, and woodpeckers woven into them, and are hung with abalone strings and long, shell-covered fringes. They served no practical use, being used solely in gift-giving associated with rites of passage, such as a girl's puberty ceremony. The continuity and stability of the tribes were expressed by baskets, which are impossible to date because the same weaves, materials, and design motifs were always employed.

Basketmaking was a social activity. Lacking the meeting houses of the men, women gathered in groups in front of their family homes to prepare reeds and grasses or when any major undertaking required someone else's help. These gatherings, like those of the men, are described as calm and cheerful. There is never any hint that there might have been urgency to complete a task; everything proceeded in an unhurried, goodnatured manner. Although it was never flaunted, some women clearly had higher status than

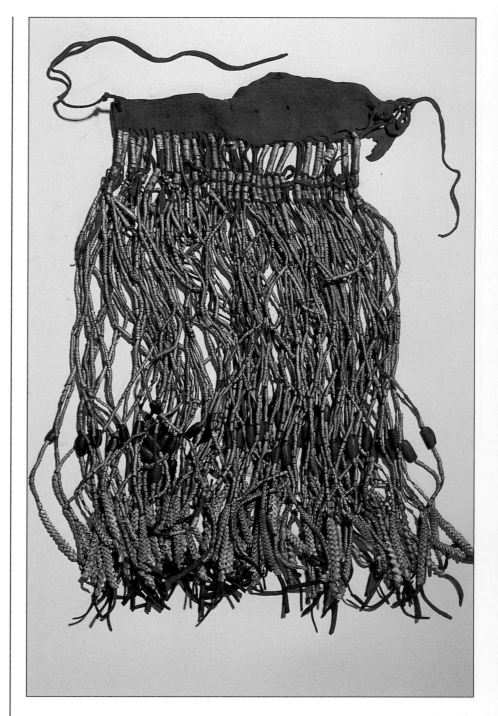

others, displaying this through shell strings of dentalia. Referred to as *kaia,* these strings were worn as necklaces, or made into collars, girdles, and pendants, and at times were sewn into the women's woven rush or cedar and willow bark aprons.

Kaia was also needed to validate a marriage, when it would be used as a form of dowry, said to represent both the status and virtue of the girl. It could also be used as compensation if another member of the tribe had been slighted. Its principal use, however, was as a standard of currency. Every trader carried an elk-horn purse containing several strings and would use these in payment for other goods when the direct exchange of products was not possible. *Kaia* would also be used in making payment to a shaman in cases of sickness where the family's own herbal remedies had proved ineffective.

Fiber apron, Wintu. Aprons of grasses, rush and fiber were worn by women throughout the central and southern California areas. The type of apron shown here is that worn by the Wintu. It is made from buckskin and cut leather strings, which are wrapped with bear grass. Red seeds and pinenut kernels have been added to the strings.

SHAMANS

Shamans, almost always women, had no powers as diviners or seers, but were concerned almost exclusively with healing rites and cures. Their power came through a dream, but this was rarely one that had been deliberately sought. The central Californian shaman was "chosen" to practice, and she had little say in whether she wanted to or not. This contrasts sharply with the dream-visions of the southern coastal tribes, which were not shamanic, but were induced by the jimson weed, or datura. These dreams formed the basis for the Toloache cult into which all young men were initiated, and visions arising from the use of this powerful narcotic were believed to control the man's mystic thought throughout adulthood.

SOUTHERN CALIFORNIA

In other respects, southern Californian life was much like that of the central area, but with a stronger emphasis on products of the sea and coastal fishing. The land was more arid, and plant products were less readily available. The Indians may have developed stronger inter-group alliances and shared culture complexes. They are reputed to have had elaborate lunar-solar calendars which were interpreted by shamans, and to have made sandpaintings in which star movements were accurately depicted. Unfortunately, we know very little about this; their culture was shattered and destroyed when the Spanish established their missions. Indeed, we know the tribes only by Mission names: the Dieguenos, from the Mission of San Diego; Gabrielenos, from the Mission of San Gabriel near Los Angeles; Luisenos, from San Luis Obispo; or Juanenos, from San Juan de Capistrano.

A few scattered tribes in Baja California escaped the mission system and survive into modern times. Their culture was a markedly conservative one, totally opposed to outside influence and very resistant to change. Typical of these people are the Seri. They had a coastal lifestyle and were dependent on the sea turtle as a food source, which they hunted from boats made of bundles of reeds. Clothing was often of swan skins, and their women bore elaborate facial tattoos and paintings that depicted their family allegiance. The most striking thing about them, in terms of Californian history, is that they refused to accept any innovation. Until the turn of the century, they still used bone- and shell-bladed spears for turtle-fishing. Anything contaminated by the hands of White men was anathema to them: they had no metal-bladed knives, kettles, tin ornaments, or beads, and chose to isolate themselves completely. Until quite recently, virtually nothing was known about their culture.

Cocopa man, Yuma woman. Personal adornment among Californian tribes was often lavished on the hair, to which both paint and feathers might be applied, as in these examples.

Feather gift basket, Pomo. The most elaborate and precious Californian baskets were produced by the Pomo as gifts and to mark rites of passage.

Feather belt, Pomo, 1875–1900. Colored feathers are woven on a milkweed fiber base to produce this belt. It would have been worn by men across one shoulder and supposed to possess power to frighten enemies: a fitting symbolic meaning for such a delicate object in a region where violence was generally abhorred.

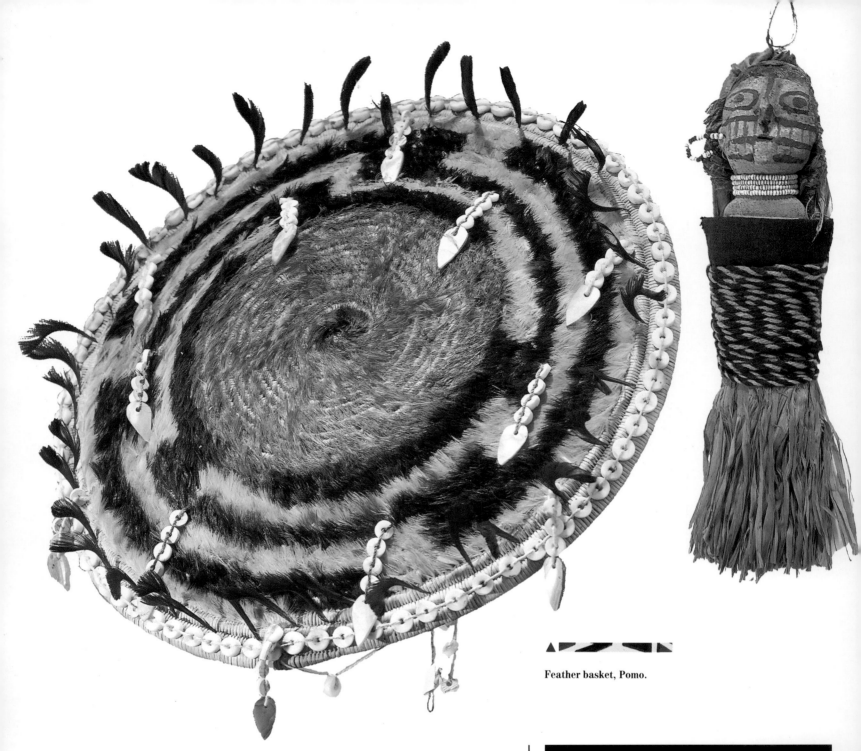

Feather basket, Pomo.

NORTHERN CALIFORNIA

In northern California the tribes had close contacts with those of the Northwest Coast of Washington and British Columbia. They traded regularly with them at the Dalles, on the Columbia River, where Californian abalone shell was a sought-after trade item. Their association with the groups of the Northwest Coast led to a greater insistence on wealth displays and a more aggressive attitude, as well as to the adoption of plank housing and the use of dugout canoes. These tribes, which include the Klamath, Modoc, Hupa, and Yurok, believed that wealth and status were things that could be equated.

Only the wealthiest families were able to sponsor the feasts at which valuable white deerskin dance costumes and red woodpecker feather head-dresses would be displayed. Such feasts might last for 20 days or more. Marriages between wealthy families created an aristocracy with a system of social class quite different from that of other tribes in California. Yet

Dance outfit, Yurok/Karok, nineteenth century. The back skirt shown here would have been worn together with an apron, and folded double to cover the woman's back and sides. It is cut from a piece of buckskin, with buckskin cut-outs wrapped in bear grass and ferns, shell-hung fringes, and abalone pendants.

▶▷◼◿◣◥◢

Mohave woman. The Mohave were distinguished by the female practice of wearing elaborate facial tattoos that indicated family and status. Although the custom was fading by the turn of the nineteenth century, there were still women living at that time who had tattoo markings.

◀◁◼◿◣◥◢

Doll, Mohave. Pottery dolls were characteristic of the Yuma and Mohave of the southern Arizona-California area. This Mohave example uses tiny seed beads, trade cloth wrapped with string, and plant fibers, and shows tattoo markings on the face.

the northern Californian tribes were still very much a part of the Californian way of life. Essentially non-aggressive, they lived a relaxed and comfortable life, with little fear of shortages and no need to defend their territorial claims.

THE DESERT WEST

California and the Desert West lands of the Great Basin are separated by the fault-block mountains of the Sierra Nevada. These are high enough to prevent rain-bearing clouds reaching the Great Basin, which is thus a semi-arid desert. It has no rivers, sparse vegetation and little animal life. In many respects, the Great Basin area is utterly desolate, yet the archaeological record indicates a human habitation that goes back to at least 9,000 B.C.

In the historic period, this land was home to the Ute, Gosiute, Paiute, Shoshone, and Bannock, whose single-family shelters were holes dug in the ground and covered by whatever meager brush they could find to act as a windbreak. They wore rabbit-skin robes, collected *piñon* nuts, hunted more frequently with a throwing-stick than they did with bow and arrow, and the only items of regular manufacture were crude baskets made from twigs. Much of their food was dug from the ground, but it was never planted. Most distasteful to the first Europeans who met them was their custom of eating such things as lizards and grasshoppers; the Europeans quickly gave them the contemptuous name "Digger Indians."

Their land was certainly harsh and difficult, but we need to remember that they and their ancestors had survived here for 11,000 years. A European explorer in the area without help would succumb within days, if not hours. These people knew the land intimately and were perfectly attuned to the subtle clues it held. Their senses of smell, sight, touch, and taste were reliable guides to the resources it offered and enabled them to dig up edible tubers in apparently featureless landscapes or to follow the scent of moisture to a distant pool of water.

We should see these Indians as model examples of how people can survive in a hostile environment without the need for sophisticated technological aids. To them, the Great Basin was never a wasteland, but contained a supply of roots, seeds, berries, nuts, and small mammals and reptiles that could be used to sustain life if one knew how to find them. They had

Hupa woman. This photograph of Alice Spot shows her wearing an elaborate costume that was the property of a wealthy family. The skirt is covered with shell attachments. She also wears a basketwork hat, typical of the central and northern Californian tribes. Behind her is a Hupa plank house.

little formal ceremonialism. The resources of their country limited any celebratory act to the individual: a few drops of rabbit blood spilled on the ground by the hunter as a way of thanks, or the offering of some braided grasses from a girl attaining puberty. Such acts indicated that the spirits were being thought of; in a region of hostility such things were important because no chances could be taken that resources would be withdrawn.

The procurement of food had to be their main concern, and when Spanish horses found their way into the area, many of the tribes considered them as just another food source. However, those in the slightly more hospitable eastern regions, such as the Ute and Shoshone, realized the potential of the animal and became equestrian. Expanding rapidly, they formed new, more powerful family groupings and began to ally themselves with other tribes, both from the Great Basin and from neighboring areas. Their culture underwent a complete transformation. They started to move onto the Plains for seasonal buffalo hunts, adopting many customs from tribes they came in contact with there. Brush-covered shelters were replaced by tepees, and rabbit-skin blankets were abandoned for deerskin shirts and heavy winter robes.

THE PLATEAU

Both the Shoshone and Ute were instrumental in the spread of horses from the Apache in the Southwest to the tribes living in the Plateau lands north of the Great Basin. This is an area of astonishing natural beauty. Calm meadows lie enclosed within the peaks of the mountains that surround the Plateau, and gentle streams meander through its high grasslands. There are mountain valleys, hot springs, and snow-covered passes. Even today, it has the quality of being an untouched land, one that has not been despoiled by the industrialist or the agriculturalist. The Cayuse, Flathead, Klikitat, Wishram, and Nez Percé lived here, together with a host of smaller tribes.

The villages of semisubterranean plank dwellings, or of lodges covered with mats made from bulrushes, were stretched in long lines along the river banks in the valley bottoms. The rivers teemed with fish, and roots and berries were plentiful. Tribes living in the mountains, who had a more nomadic lifestyle, came regularly to the villages to trade furs for dried salmon. In common with California, there were no societies of warriors and little aggression between the various groups. They intermarried and incorporated elements from each other's cultures. They traveled widely, visiting other people whose languages they did not speak, but where they were made welcome and shared in ceremonies, dances, and traditions, using a sign language that all understood.

Bag, Wasco, late nineteenth century. Wasco weavers of the Lower Columbia River used native hemp in making highly characteristic baskets with stylized head designs. This stylization had an enduring quality and is seen on baskets from both the pre- and post-contact periods.

Hat, Karok/Yurok.

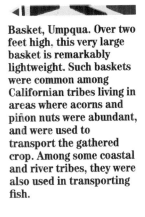

Basket, Umpqua. Over two feet high, this very large basket is remarkably lightweight. Such baskets were common among Californian tribes living in areas where acorns and piñon nuts were abundant, and were used to transport the gathered crop. Among some coastal and river tribes, they were also used in transporting fish.

Paiute women, Kaibab Plateau, c1873. These two women are wearing basketwork hats and are carrying very large burden baskets, using tumplines drawn across the chest to support the weight. They hold flat basket trays, used when winnowing piñon nuts.

Basketry hat, Paiute. The Paiute tribes made close-woven basketry hats with a heavy rim and characteristic form. These were often undecorated, but some had darker patterns woven into them. It is clear the Paiute, although frequently living at or near subsistence level, felt that esthetic considerations were important.

A MIX OF CULTURES

These people borrowed freely from one another, and the Plateau was remarkable in the mix of ideas and beliefs that were demonstrated. There are grave markers analogous to the totems of the British Columbia and Alaska coast; birchbark containers similar to those made in the Subarctic; and porcupine quill embroidery showing influences from the Athapascan tribes of interior British Columbia. The people of the Plateau were excellent woodcarvers, skilled in weaving rushes and grasses into mats and bags, and adept at using stone, sheep's horn, and antler in making bowls, ladles, and other household items. Even their clothing reflected this skill, and women wore basketwork hats and buckskin dresses covered with elaborate designs, originally applied with seeds and shells, but later with trade beads.

Most importantly, they sat at the hub of a great trade network serving California and the Northwest Coast, and extending into the Plains. Goods were transported in dugout canoes to the Dalles trade center, where furs and skins could be exchanged for Californian abalone shells and other coastal products. Mountain passes provided access to trade for Plateau groups who lived a nomadic hunting life, and they would bring their goods down to the villages and from there to the Dalles. Other passes led east and to contact with the Blackfoot and the Crow. This contact introduced many ideas to the Nez Percé and Cayusa, whose cultures show strong Plains influence.

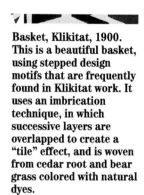

Basket, Klikitat, 1900. This is a beautiful basket, using stepped design motifs that are frequently found in Klikitat work. It uses an imbrication technique, in which successive layers are overlapped to create a "tile" effect, and is woven from cedar root and bear grass colored with natural dyes.

When horses were traded from the Spanish settlements of the Southwest in the early 1700s by the Ute, Shoshone, Comanche, and Kiowa, it may have been the Nez Percé and Cayusa who passed them on to the tribes of the Northern Plains. The Plateau environment was ideally suited to the tough Spanish horses. The herds flourished, and both the Cayusa and the Nez Percé quickly established themselves as horse raisers and breeders. Through selective breeding, they developed the famous dappled pony that we know as the Appaloosa. Soon the Nez Percé villages in the breathtakingly beautiful Wallowa Valley were distinguished by literally thousands of horses that grazed the rich grasslands.

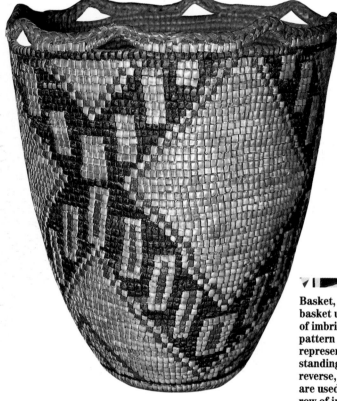

Basket, Klikitat. This basket uses the technique of imbrication. The pattern here is a representation of five standing people. On the reverse, darker grasses are used to form a double row of interlocking diamonds.

Small basket, Klikitat, before 1842. This tiny basket is just over 2½ inches (6.5 cms) high. It is woven from grass, and may have been used for storing small items, or was perhaps simply a demonstration of its maker's skill.

Edna Kash-Kash, Cayusa, c1900. The Cayusa lived in relative comfort, and were noted for the richness of their costume. Edna Kash-Kash wears a particularly fine buckskin dress with an elaborate beaded yoke, and a tightly woven basketwork hat.

THE FLIGHT OF THE NEZ PERCÉ

It was an idyllic existence, in a land of plenty. Winters might be cold, but the mountain air was fresh and revitalizing. Warm buffalo robes were being brought back from the grasslands to the east, obtained in exchange for horses. Other tribes were friendly, coming into the Nez Percé villages regularly and sharing in their feasts and dances. This was not to last. In the 1850s, White settlers began arriving in the Plateau lands and demanding the removal of the Indian tribes from the meadows to make room for settlement and cattle grazing. There were some violent outbreaks, and Chief Joseph of the Nez Percé attempted to lead his people to sanctuary in Canada. This was an heroic flight in which he led the tribe over 1,300 miles (800 kilometers) through snow blizzards, evading four separate military columns sent to intercept them, before finally being stopped just 30 miles (50 kilometers) from the border.

Joseph's Nez Percé were removed to Indian Territory (Oklahoma), other tribes of the region were herded onto small reservations, and the Plateau became home to White cattlemen. Yet there is a permanent Indian presence. In the distant mythological past, Coyote journeyed through these peaceful mountain valleys and came to a village ruled by a woman. He asked her what she was doing. She replied she was teaching the people to live well, to share with each other in friendship and trade, and to establish villages of fine houses along the rivers. Coyote went with her into the mountains, where he turned her into a rock so that she might watch over the people always. One can look up into the mountains and see the woman chief, Tsagigla'lal, waiting patiently for her lessons to be heeded.

Chief Joseph, Nez Percé. Joseph believed that both, Indian and White could live together and learn from one another, with neither losing their dignity or giving up their beliefs. Early explorers found Joseph to be amiable and friendly, always willing to offer help. Joseph's trust was, however, betrayed.

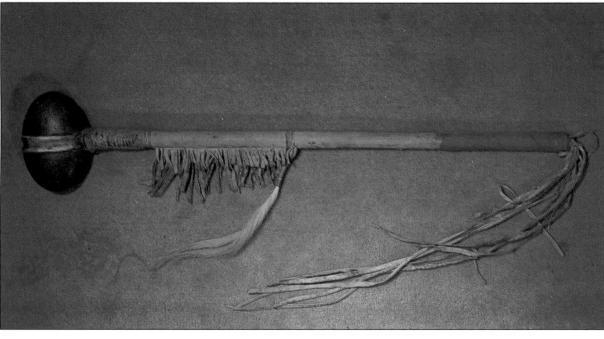

War club, Cayusa, before 1850. A dark stone head is attached to a wooden shaft by a rawhide wrapping that has been heat shrunk to fix the head securely in place. The shaft is wrapped in deer skin with a cut fringe and red trade cloth. Of particular interest is the scalp of European hair.

Cornhusk bag, Nez Percé.
Two sides of the same bag.
The Nez Percé originally
wove similar bags from
bear grass, but by the late
nineteenth century these
had been replaced entirely
by bags woven from the
inner parts of cornhusks.
Such bags were a valuable
trade item, and were also
used for the storage of
roots and berries.

Octopus bag, Plateau.
Such bags – so-named
from the "tentacle" shape
of the fringe – were
important trade items.
These bags follow the

Index

•••••••••••

Picture Credits

BW Ben Whittick, Museum of New Mexico. BS B. Saal, Hamburgisches Museum für Völkerkunde. WC Will Channing, Earth Circle Foundation. MN Museum of New Mexico. NM Navajo Museum. PK Staatliche Museen Preussischer Kulturbesitz, Berlin. UM Übersee Museum, Bremen. MC National Museum of Civilization, Ottawa. BM British Museum. IW Ian West Collection. DL Deutsches Ledermuseum, Offenbach. WM Woolaroc. WK W. Knust, Kuprianoff Collection, Staatliche Museen für Naturkunde und Vorgeschichte, Oldenburg. RF The Robert and Francis Flaherty Study Center, Claremont, California. GP Museum of the Great Plains, Lawton, Oklahoma. VD V. Didoni, Linden Museum, Stuttgart. OT Osage Tribal Museum, Pawhuska, Oklahoma. EC Edward Curtis. BC British Columbia Archives and Record Service, Victoria. TB Thomas Burke Memorial, Washington State Museum. DB De Bry. SN Smithsonian Institution, National Museum of the American Indian. SI Smithsonian Institution, National Archives, SA Smithsonian Institution, National Museum of American Art. CB Carl Bodmer. HS Hilliers. GC George Caitlin.

All other pictures come from private collections. Numbers refer to sequence in chapter.

Introduction, Chapter 1: Pouch PK; A. Pueblo BW; San I. pot WC; A. pot WC; Zuni HS/SI; H. dancers SI; Kachina WC; A. pot 2 BS; P.–P. women SI; saddle bag WC; G. dancers SI; bridle SI; blanket WC; sandpainting NM; weaver MN; N. blanket 2 WC. Chapter 2: labrets SI; bowl WC; parka 1, 2 BS; mittens UM; bag UM; goggles UM; charm UM; woman SI; visor BS; coat BS; Chagamiut 1, 2 SI; Otterman WK; ladle WK; dress/leggings BS; dress BS; Kutchin SI; quiver BS; club WK; bag 2 MS; hood BS; scraper MC; mittens 2 MS; baskets BM; snowshoes IW; sheath BM; coat 2 SI; Naskapi RF; mocassins 2 DL; box BS; pouch 1, 2, 3 BM. Chapter 3: camp GP; Kiowa GC/SA; knife/sheath VD; robe SI; mocassins VD; lodges SI; Pawnee 1, 2, 3 GC/SA; pipe VD; Osage man SI; gorget WM; Kansa GC/SA; Omaha GC/SA; robe 2 VD; bag OT; lodge SI; girl GC/SA; awl BM; girls SI; cradleboard BS; Comanche GP; parfleche VD; dancer CB/SI; hoop VD; pipes VD; pouch PK; Blackfoot GC/SA; leggings VD; shield MB. Chapter 4: house SI; mask UM; daughter EC/BC; basket 1, 2 BM; dance EC/BC; dancer EC/BC; r. mask BM; ivory/bone BS; p. mask BM; girl EC/BC; hat BM; club BM; village BC; apron TB; dolls UM; knife BS; mask 2 WK; p. hat SI; hat 2 BS. Chapter 5: mask SI; woman DB/SI; house SI; baskets all BM; mocassins 1, 2 BM; women SI; Peoria GC/SA; Creek SI; bag 1, 2 SN; village SI; mocassins 2 BM; sash WC; club BM; Iroquois SI; pouch 2 VD; p. bags BM; straps BM; cord BM; mocassins BS; club 2 SI; y. pouch BM; sash 2, 3 BM; Chippewa GC/SA; feathers SI; club 3 VD. Chapter 6: girl SI; ornament BM; string BM; necklace BM; apron UM; man SI; woman SI; f. basket 2 WC; belt SI; Mohave SI; doll BM; dress WC; Hupa SI; basket SI; Umpqua BM; hat BM; Paiutes SI; K. basket WC; K. basket 2 BM; mini basket BM; Joseph SI; Cayusa SI; Nez P. bag 1, 2 BM; octopus b. 1, 2 BM; blanket SI; men & w. SI.